A BALANCED MATHEMATICS PROGRAM INTEGRATING SCIENCE AND LANGUAGE ARTS

Discovery
Assignment
Book

THIRD EDITION

KENDALL/HUNT PUBLISHING COMPANY
4050 Westmark Drive   Dubuque, Iowa   52002

A TIMS® Curriculum
University of Illinois at Chicago

MATH TRAILBLAZERS®

Dedication

This book is dedicated to
the children and teachers who
let us see the magic in their classrooms
and to our families who wholeheartedly
supported us while we searched for
ways to make it happen.

The TIMS Project

 UIC The University of Illinois
at Chicago

The original edition was based on work supported by the National Science Foundation under grant No. MDR 9050226 and the University of Illinois at Chicago. Any opinions, findings, and conclusions or recommendations expressed in this publication are those of the authors and do not necessarily reflect the views of the granting agencies.

Printed in the United States of America

1 2 3 4 5 6 7 8 9 10   11 10 09 08 07

Table of Contents

Additional student pages may be found in the *Unit Resource Guide, Student Guide,* or the *Adventure Book.*

Table of Contents

Additional student pages may be found in the *Unit Resource Guide, Student Guide,* or the *Adventure Book.*

Table of Contents

Additional student pages may be found in the *Unit Resource Guide, Student Guide,* or the *Adventure Book.*

LETTER TO PARENTS

Dear Parents,

Math Trailblazers® is based on the ideas that mathematics is best learned through solving many different kinds of problems and that all children deserve a challenging mathematics curriculum. The program provides a careful balance of concepts and skills. Traditional arithmetic skills and procedures are covered through their repeated use in problems and through distributed practice. *Math Trailblazers,* however, offers much more. Students using this program will become proficient problem solvers, will know when and how to apply the mathematics they have

learned, and will be able to clearly communicate their mathematical knowledge. Computation, measurement, geometry, data collection and analysis, estimation, graphing, patterns and relationships, mental arithmetic, and simple algebraic ideas are all an integral part of the curriculum. They will see connections between the mathematics learned in school and the mathematics used in everyday life. And, they will enjoy and value the work they do in mathematics.

The *Discovery Assignment Book* is only one component of *Math Trailblazers.* Additional material and lessons are contained in the *Student Guide,* the *Adventure Book*, and in the teacher's *Unit Resource Guides.* If you have questions about the program, we encourage you to speak with your child's teacher.

This curriculum was built around national recommendations for improving mathematics instruction in American schools and the research that supported those recommendations. The first edition was extensively tested with thousands of children in dozens of classrooms over five years of development. In preparing the second and third editions, we have benefited from the comments and suggestions of hundreds of teachers and children who have used the curriculum. *Math Trailblazers* reflects our view of a complete and well-balanced mathematics program that will prepare children for the 21st century—a world in which mathematical skills will be important in most occupations and mathematical reasoning will be essential for acting as an informed citizen in a democratic society. We hope that you enjoy this exciting approach to learning mathematics and that you watch your child's mathematical abilities grow throughout the year.

Philip Wagreich

Philip Wagreich
Professor, Department of Mathematics, Statistics, and Computer Science
Director, Institute for Mathematics and Science Education
Teaching Integrated Mathematics and Science (TIMS) Project
University of Illinois at Chicago

Unit 1

Populations and Samples

	Student Guide	Discovery Assignment Book	Adventure Book	Unit Resource Guide*
Lesson 1				
Eyelets	●			●
Lesson 2				
Review: Representing Data				●
Lesson 3				
Analyzing Data	●			
Lesson 4				
A Matter of Survival			●	
Lesson 5				
Searching the Forest	●			●
Lesson 6				
Practice Problems	●			

Unit Resource Guide pages are from the teacher materials.

Unit 1 Home Practice

PART 1 Addition and Subtraction

Solve the following problems in your head.

A. 30 + 90 = _____

B. 50 + 60 = _____

C. 160 − 90 = _____

D. 148 − 50 = _____

E. 240 + 80 = _____

F. 100 − 32 = _____

G. 650 + 250 = _____

H. 732 + 632 = _____

I. 389 + 11 = _____

On another sheet of paper, explain how you solved two of the problems in your head.

PART 2 Variables and Values in Your Home

1. A. David asks each of his family members what his or her favorite vegetable is. Is he collecting data on a numerical or categorical variable?

  B. List four possible values for this variable.

2. A. Alexis asks her classmates how long it takes them to get to school. What variable is she studying? Is it numerical or categorical?

  B. List four possible values for this variable. (*Hint:* How long does it take you to get to school? How long does it take your friends?)

3. A. Brandon asks his friends what type of sandwiches they are going to order at the fast-food restaurant. Is he collecting data on a numerical or categorical variable?

  B. List four possible values for this variable.

PART 3 Finding the Median
Find the median for each set of data given below. Show how you decided.

1. Roberto, David, Nila, Lee Yah, and Romesh compared the number of videos their families own. Roberto owns 47 videos while David only owns 4. Nila owns 23 videos, Lee Yah owns 18 videos, and Romesh owns 15 videos. What is the median number of videos? (*Hint:* First list the number of videos owned by each family in order from smallest to largest. You should list five numbers.)

2. Brandon compared five different types of basketball shoes. His favorite brand has 24 eyelets. His least favorite has 32 eyelets. Two brands have pairs of shoes with 20 eyelets. Another brand has 28 eyelets. What is the median number of eyelets? (*Hint:* List the number 20 twice since two pairs of shoes have 20 eyelets.)

3. There are seven people in Felicia's family. Four members of her family have 5 pairs of shoes. Two members of her family have 3 pairs of shoes. Her mother has 15 pairs of shoes. What is the median number of pairs of shoes in Felicia's household? What is the mode? (*Hint:* List the number 5 four times since four members have 5 pairs of shoes. List the number 3 twice.)

4. Four people in David's family celebrate birthdays in September. David buys 4 cards. The card for his mother costs $2.25. The cards for his two brothers are $1.25 and $1.40. The card for his cousin is $1.50. What is the median price of the birthday cards?

5. What is the median height in your household? How did you decide?

PART 4   Addition and Subtraction Practice

Solve the following problems using paper and pencil only. Estimate to make sure your answers are reasonable.

A. $75 + 39 =$

B. $167 + 74 =$

C. $254 - 118 =$

D. $7046 + 856 =$

E. $9233 - 560 =$

F. $8570 + 2545 =$

G. $5649 - 1850 =$

H. $5503 + 7098 =$

I. $6800 - 4874 =$

PART 5   Number of Windows

Brandon collected data on the number of windows in each room of his home. His data is shown below. Make a bar graph of Brandon's data on a piece of graph paper. Label the horizontal axis with the variable, Number of Windows.

Number of Windows	Number of Rooms
0	0
1	2
2	3
3	0
4	1

1. What is the most common number of windows in the rooms in Brandon's home?

2. How many windows are in Brandon's home altogether?

PART 6 Solving Problems

Choose an appropriate method to solve each of the following problems. For some questions you may need to find an exact answer, while for others you may only need an estimate. For each question, you may choose to use paper and pencil, mental math, or a calculator. Be prepared to tell the class how you solved each problem.

1. Michael's mother baked 3 dozen cookies for Michael's birthday party. If seven friends are coming to the party, how many cookies can each child have if they share the cookies equally? (*Hint:* Don't forget to give Michael some cookies.)

2. The gym teacher bought 50 balls for the high school. He bought 35 tennis balls that cost 60¢ each. The rest of the balls were golf balls that cost $1.25 each. How much money did he spend altogether?

3. Mr. Moreno went to Springfield for a four-day weekend. He stayed at a hotel for three nights. The bill was $267. What was the rate for each night?

4. Irma is shopping with her cousin Maria, who recently got married. As a wedding gift, Maria received a $100 gift certificate at a department store. She finds the following items that she wants to buy: a comforter for $48, two pillows for $23 each, a waffle maker for $39, three picture frames for $5.95 each, and a cookbook for $12. Since she only has $100 to spend, make a list of the items she can purchase with her gift certificate. Explain your thinking.

Unit 2

Big Numbers

	Student Guide	Discovery Assignment Book	Adventure Book	Unit Resource Guide*
Lesson 1				
Reading and Writing Big Numbers	●	●		
Lesson 2				
Facts I Know	●	●		●
Lesson 3				
The Base-Ten Number System				●
Lesson 4				
The Chinese Abacus	●			●
Lesson 5				
Multiplication	●			●
Lesson 6				
Estimating Products	●			
Lesson 7				
Sand Reckoning			●	
Lesson 8				
Exponents and Large Numbers	●			
Lesson 9				
Stack Up				●
Lesson 10				
Portfolios	●			

Unit Resource Guide pages are from the teacher materials.

⬤ Unit 2 Home Practice

PART 1 Triangle Flash Cards: 5s and 10s

Study for the quiz on the multiplication and division facts for the 5s and 10s. Take home your *Triangle Flash Cards: 5s* and *10s* and your list of facts you need to study.

Ask a family member to choose one flash card at a time. To quiz you on a multiplication fact, he or she should cover the corner containing the highest number. (The highest number on each card is lightly shaded.) This number will be the answer to two multiplication facts. Multiply the two uncovered numbers.

$5 \times 4 = ?$

$4 \times 5 = ?$

To quiz you on a division fact, your family member can cover the number in the square. Then you use the two uncovered numbers to solve a division fact. Your family member can then cover the number inside the circle to quiz you on a related division fact.

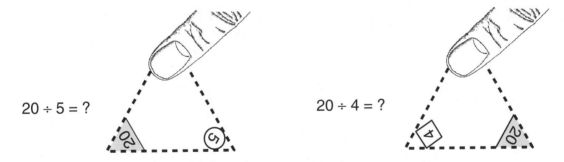

$20 \div 5 = ?$ $20 \div 4 = ?$

Ask your family member to mix up the multiplication and division facts. He or she should sometimes cover the highest number, sometimes cover the circled number, and sometimes cover the number in the square.

Your teacher will tell you when the quiz on the 5s and 10s will be given.

PART 2 Numbers in the Hundreds and Thousands

1. Number the line below from 0 to 10,000. Skip count by 1000s.

0

Read each of the facts about the United States below. Then make a tick mark on the number line above to show where each number falls on the line. Label the tick mark with the appropriate letter.

A. The highest bridge over water in the world—1053 feet—is in Colorado. It is the suspension bridge over the Royal Gorge of the Arkansas River.

B. Mount Katahdin is the highest spot in Maine—5268 feet. This mountain is the first place in the entire United States to get hit with sunlight when the sun rises in the morning.

C. The world's tallest living redwood tree on record stands 367 feet tall. Redwood trees are native to California.

2. Without actually finding exact answers to these problems, give the number of digits in the answer. Explain how you know.

A. 512 + 369

B. 843 − 776

C. 2190 + 8756

D. 15 × 65

E. 4589 − 637

PART 3 Multiplication Practice

1. Solve the following problems using paper and pencil only. Estimate to make sure your answers make sense.

   A. $24 \times 6 =$ **B.** $257 \times 4 =$ **C.** $4795 \times 5 =$ **D.** $3809 \times 8 =$

   E. $12 \times 45 =$ **F.** $30 \times 62 =$ **G.** $79 \times 48 =$ **H.** $95 \times 18 =$

2. Solve the following problems. Choose an appropriate method: mental math, paper and pencil, or a calculator. *Hint:* Sometimes drawing a picture of a problem can help you solve it.

   A. Jessie's mother is shopping in a sports store. Socks are on sale for $2.95 for 3 pairs. If she has $20, how many pairs of socks can she buy?

   B. Lin's father purchased a brand new car. His car payments are $318 monthly for 4 years. After 4 years, how much will he have paid for his car?

   C. Last year Mr. Moreno bought two cans of soda from the machine each day at school. This year he decided to drink water instead. If one can of soda costs 65¢, will Mr. Moreno save more or less than $100 in one school year? (A school year has about 180 school days.)

PART 4 Solving Problems

Solve the following problems. Choose an appropriate method for each: mental math, paper and pencil, or a calculator. Explain your solutions.

1. A mouse can have a litter of as many as 16 pups. A mouse can have up to 6 litters each year. About how many mice, at most, can one mouse produce in 6 years?

2. The U.S. government recommends that girls between the ages of 11 and 14 consume 2400 calories of food a day. Boys of the same age should consume 2800 calories.

   A. A boy follows these guidelines. Will he consume more or less than 25,000 calories in one week?

   B. In one week, how many more calories should a boy eat than a girl?

3. One of the longest running Broadway musical plays ran for about 15 years. On average, there were 409 performances each year.

   A. About how many performances were there in all over the 15 years?

   B. About how many performances were there each month?

Writing Big Numbers

Complete the table. An example is shown.

Standard Form	Expanded Form	Word Form
33,128	30,000 + 3000 + 100 + 20 + 8	Thirty-three thousand, one hundred twenty-eight
1,355,227		
	20,000,000 + 2,000,000 + 400,000 + 18,000 + 900 + 60 + 5	
		Fifty-seven million, two hundred fourteen thousand
165,998,247		
		Twenty-nine billion, two hundred seventy-three million, nine hundred ninety-eight thousand, one hundred five

Population Lines

Number this line from 0 to 100,000. Skip count by 10,000s.

0

Number this line from 0 to 1,000,000. Some numbers have been written for you.

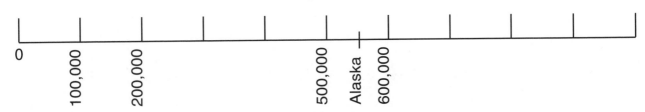

0   100,000   200,000   500,000 Alaska 600,000

Number this line from 0 to 10,000,000. Skip count by millions.

0

Number this line from 0 to 100,000,000. Skip count by ten millions.

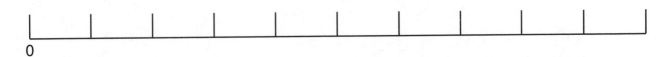

0

Spin and Read Number Game Spinners

Spinner 1

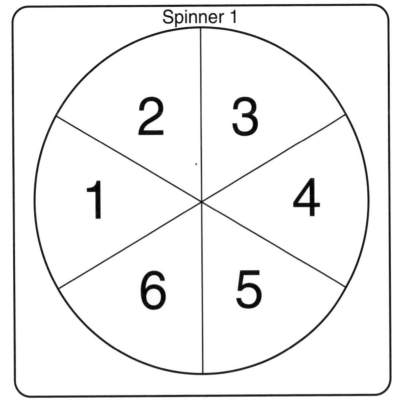

Spinner 2

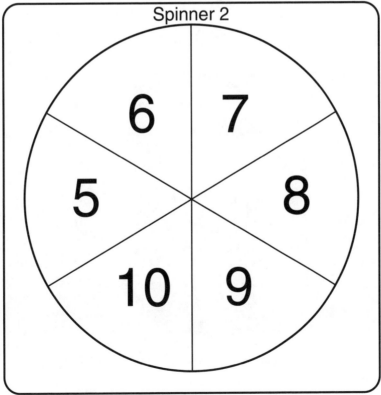

Place Value Chart

Trillions			Billions			Millions			Thousands			Ones		

Triangle Flash Cards: 5s

- Work with a partner. Each partner cuts out the flash cards below.
- Your partner chooses one card at a time and covers one corner.
- To quiz you on a multiplication fact, your partner covers the shaded number. Multiply the two uncovered numbers.
- To quiz you on a division fact, your partner covers the number in the square or the number in the circle. Solve a division fact with the two uncovered numbers.
- Divide the cards into three piles: those facts you know and can answer quickly, those you can figure out with a strategy, and those you need to learn.
- Practice the last two piles again. Then make a list of the facts you need to practice at home.
- Repeat the directions for your partner.

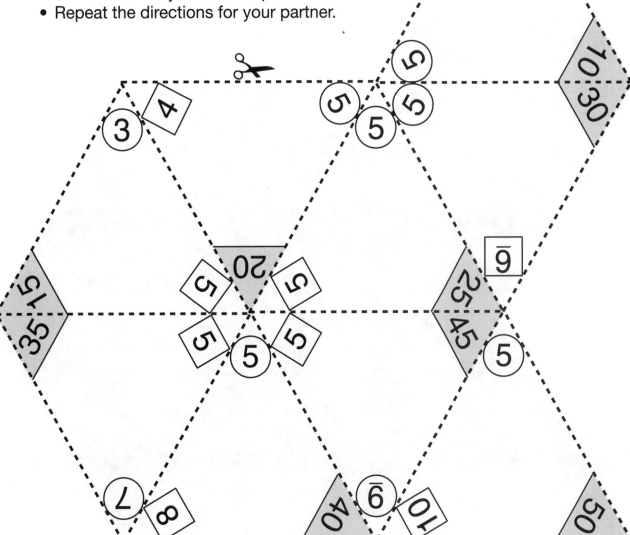

Triangle Flash Cards: 10s

- Work with a partner. Each partner cuts out the flash cards below.
- Your partner chooses one card at a time and covers one corner.
- To quiz you on a multiplication fact, your partner covers the shaded number. Multiply the two uncovered numbers.
- To quiz you on a division fact, your partner covers the number in the square or the number in the circle. Solve a division fact with the two uncovered numbers.
- Divide the cards into three piles: those facts you know and can answer quickly, those you can figure out with a strategy, and those you need to learn.
- Practice the last two piles again. Then make a list of the facts you need to practice at home.
- Repeat the directions for your partner.

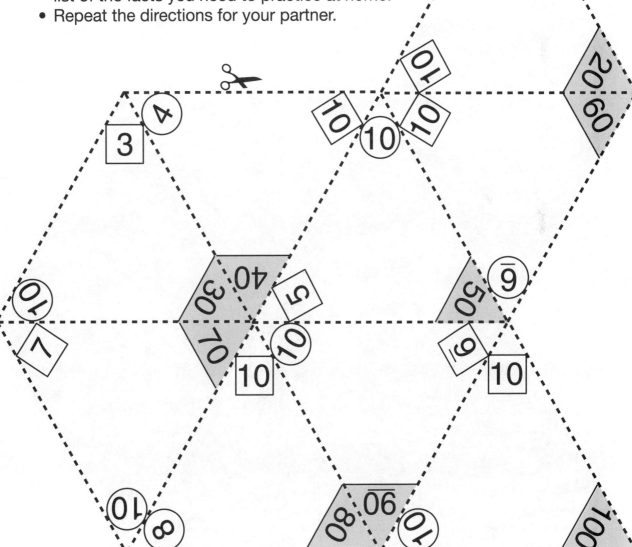

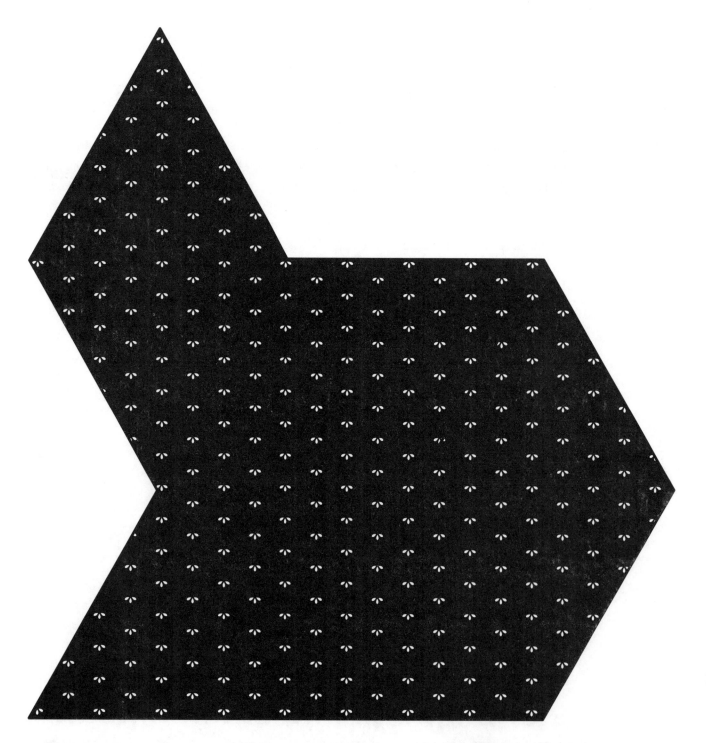

Unit 3

Fractions and Ratios

	Student Guide	Discovery Assignment Book	Adventure Book	Unit Resource Guide*
Lesson 1				
Wholes and Parts	●	●		●
Lesson 2				
Fraction Sentences	●			
Lesson 3				
Equivalent Fractions	●	●		
Lesson 4				
Comparing Fractions	●			
Lesson 5				
Using Ratios	●			●
Lesson 6				
Distance vs. Time	●			●
Lesson 7				
Speedy Problems	●			

Unit Resource Guide pages are from the teacher materials.

Unit 3 Home Practice

PART 1 *Triangle Flash Cards: 2s and 3s*

Study for the quiz on the multiplication and division facts for the 2s and 3s. Take home your *Triangle Flash Cards: 2s* and *3s* and your list of facts you need to study.

Ask a family member to choose one flash card at a time. To quiz you on a multiplication fact, he or she should cover the corner containing the highest number. Multiply the two uncovered numbers.

To quiz you on a division fact, your partner can cover one of the smaller numbers. One of the smaller numbers on each card is circled. The other has a square around it. Use the two uncovered numbers to solve a division fact.

Now mix up the multiplication and division facts. Your partner should sometimes cover the highest number, sometimes cover the circled number, and sometimes cover the number in the square.

Your teacher will tell you when the quiz on the 2s and 3s will be given.

PART 2 Rounding Numbers

Drawing number lines (or just thinking of number lines) may help you with Questions 1 and 2.

1. Round the following numbers to the nearest hundred.

   A. 213   **B.** 589   **C.** 88

   D. 1486   **E.** 2815   **F.** 5987

2. Round the following to the nearest thousand.

   A. 1286   **B.** 2815   **C.** 5987

   D. 1099   **E.** 1909   **F.** 21,643

PART 3 Fractions

1. Name a fraction between $\frac{1}{6}$ and 1. _____

2. Name a fraction between $\frac{1}{3}$ and 1. _____

3. Name a fraction with a denominator of 4 that is between 0 and 1. _____

4. Name a fraction greater than $\frac{1}{2}$ with a denominator of 8. _____

5. Name a fraction between $\frac{6}{8}$ and 1. _____

6. Which is greater:

   A. $\frac{1}{10}$ or $\frac{1}{12}$? _____

   B. $\frac{5}{8}$ or $\frac{3}{8}$? _____

   C. $\frac{7}{6}$ or 1? _____

   D. $\frac{1}{2}$ or $\frac{8}{10}$? _____

PART 4 Number Operations

1. Use paper and pencil to solve the following problems. Show your work on a separate sheet of paper. Estimate to make sure your answers are reasonable.

   A. $18 \times 36 =$ _____

   B. $7430 + 578 =$ _____

   C. $8032 - 725 =$ _____

   D. $623 \times 7 =$ _____

   E. $3419 + 7834 =$ _____

   F. $2950 \times 5 =$ _____

2. Find the amount of change each person will receive in the following problems. For each, name the least number of coins and bills. Estimate to make sure your answers are reasonable.

   A. Manny buys a hamburger for $3.99, a baked potato for $1.79, and a drink for $1.29. He gives the salesclerk a $10 bill. How much change will he receive?

   B. Lin buys 3 gallons of bubble bath at $3.39 each. If Lin gives the salesclerk a $20 bill, how much change will she receive?

PART 5 Exercising at the Gym
You will need a piece of graph paper to complete this part.

Irma's mother exercises on a stair-step machine for 18 minutes. She exercises at the same rate for the entire time. The following data table shows how many calories she burned at various times.

Time T	Calories Burned C
1	9
5	45
10	90
12	108
18	162

1. Make a point graph of the data on a piece of graph paper. Graph time on the horizontal axis. Be sure to label the axes and to give your graph a title.

2. Use a ruler to fit a line to the points.

3. About how many calories did Irma's mother burn after 15 minutes? How did you decide?

4. About how long did it take her to burn 100 calories? How did you decide?

5. **A.** Choose a point on the graph and use it to write a ratio of calories burned to time taken. (Be sure to include units.)

   B. Write two more ratios equal to the ratio in Question 5A.

   C. If Irma's mother exercised at the same rate for 30 minutes on the stair-step machine, how many calories would she burn? Explain your solution.

FRACTIONS AND RATIOS

Name _____ Date _____

PART 6 A Fraction More

1. Complete the following number sentences. The Number Lines for Fractohoppers chart you completed in Lesson 3 or the chart in Lesson 4 of the *Student Guide* may help you solve some of the problems.

   A. $\frac{1}{3} = \frac{2}{n}$

   B. $\frac{9}{12} = \frac{n}{4}$

   C. $\frac{2}{6} = \frac{n}{12}$

   D. $\frac{5}{8} = \frac{15}{n}$

   E. $\frac{20}{70} = \frac{n}{7}$

   F. $\frac{7}{9} = \frac{n}{36}$

   G. $\frac{3}{5} = \frac{n}{25}$

   H. $\frac{4}{40} = \frac{1}{n}$

   I. $\frac{2}{3} = \frac{8}{n}$

2. Write each mixed number as an improper fraction.

   A. $1\frac{1}{4}$

   B. $5\frac{2}{3}$

   C. $2\frac{7}{8}$

   D. $3\frac{3}{5}$

3. Write each improper fraction as a mixed number.

   A. $\frac{9}{4}$

   B. $\frac{20}{6}$

   C. $\frac{21}{2}$

   D. $\frac{23}{12}$

4. Put each of the following sets of fractions in order from smallest to largest.

   A. $\frac{9}{5}, \frac{9}{10}, \frac{9}{2}, \frac{9}{12}$

   B. $\frac{5}{6}, \frac{8}{7}, \frac{7}{12}, \frac{1}{8}$

   C. $\frac{6}{6}, \frac{3}{6}, \frac{10}{6}, \frac{2}{6}$

   D. $\frac{3}{20}, \frac{3}{2}, \frac{9}{11}, \frac{9}{16}$

Triangle Flash Cards: 2s

- Work with a partner. Each partner cuts out the flash cards below.
- Your partner chooses one card at a time and covers one corner.
- To quiz you on a multiplication fact, your partner covers the shaded number. Multiply the two uncovered numbers.
- To quiz you on a division fact, your partner covers the number in the square or the number in the circle. Solve a division fact with the two uncovered numbers.
- Divide the cards into three piles: those facts you know and can answer quickly, those you can figure out with a strategy, and those you need to learn.
- Practice the last two piles again. Then make a list of the facts you need to practice at home.
- Repeat the directions for your partner.

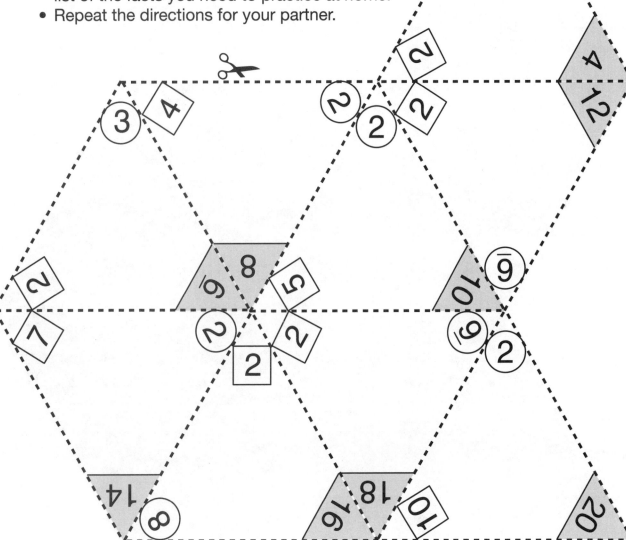

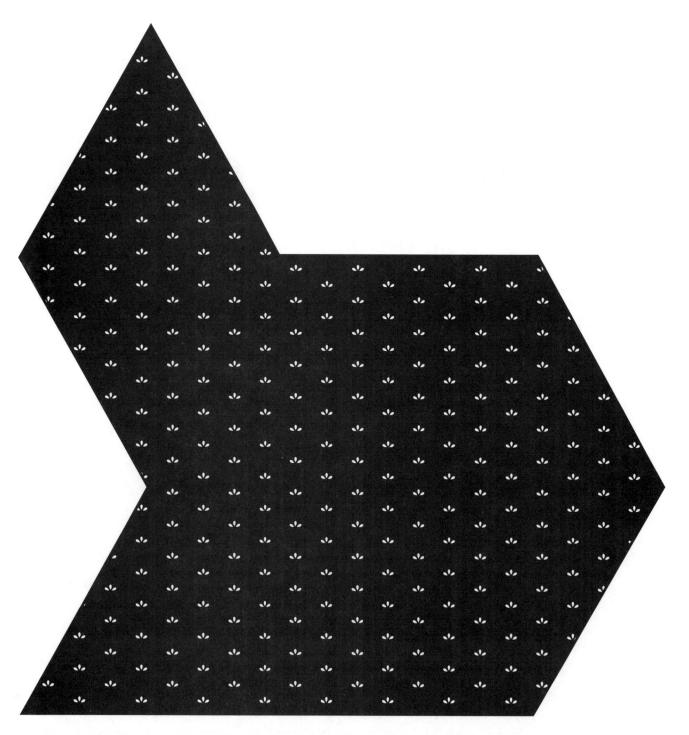

Triangle Flash Cards: 3s

- Work with a partner. Each partner cuts out the flash cards below.
- Your partner chooses one card at a time and covers one corner.
- To quiz you on a multiplication fact, your partner covers the shaded number. Multiply the two uncovered numbers.
- To quiz you on a division fact, your partner covers the number in the square or the number in the circle. Solve a division fact with the two uncovered numbers.
- Divide the cards into three piles: those facts you know and can answer quickly, those you can figure out with a strategy, and those you need to learn.
- Practice the last two piles again. Then make a list of the facts you need to practice at home.
- Repeat the directions for your partner.

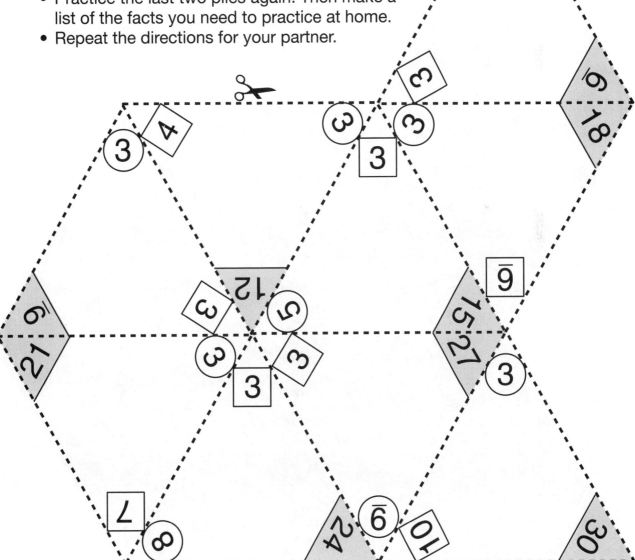

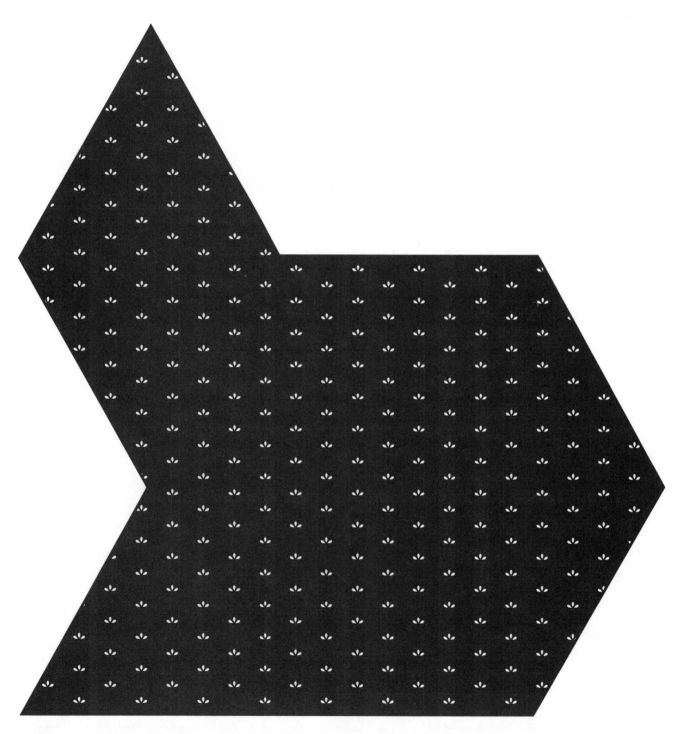

Pattern Block Record Sheet

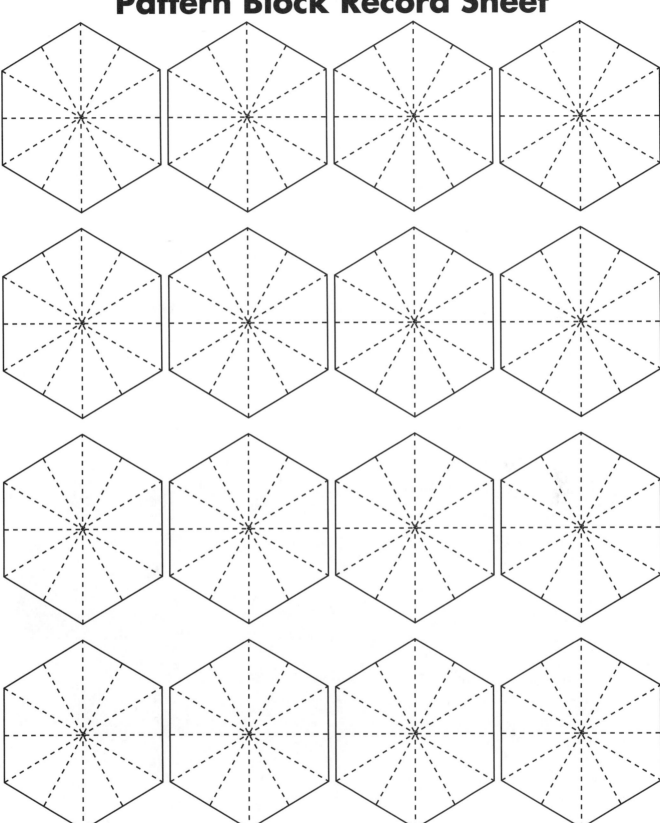

Homework: Wholes and Parts

1. If the red trapezoid is one whole, shade the following fractions.

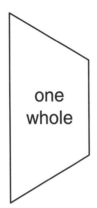

one
whole

A. $\frac{5}{6}$ 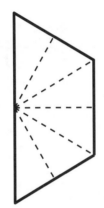   **B.** $\frac{1}{3}$ 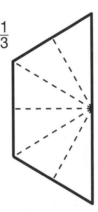   **C.** $\frac{5}{3}$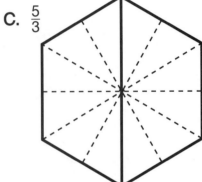

2. If the blue rhombus is one whole, shade the following fractions.

one
whole

A. $\frac{3}{4}$ 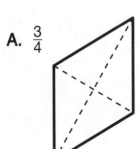   **B.** $\frac{11}{4}$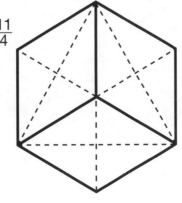

Name _____ Date _____

3. If the yellow hexagon is one whole, shade the following fractions.

one whole

A. $\frac{3}{4}$

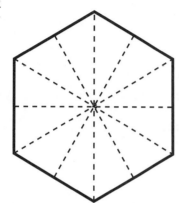

B. $\frac{9}{12}$

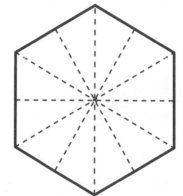

C. $\frac{5}{12}$

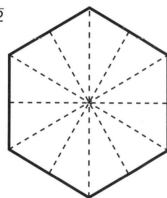

D. $1\frac{5}{6}$

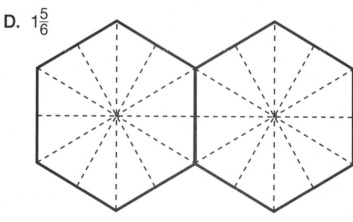

E. $\frac{2}{3}$

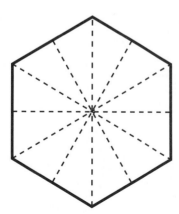

F. $\frac{7}{4}$

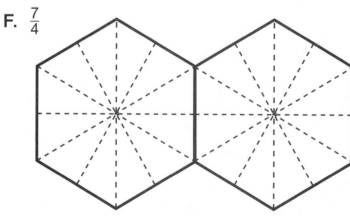

Wholes and Parts

Number Lines for Fractohoppers

To study fractohoppers, we need number lines divided into equal parts. Prepare each number line to show the hops of fractohoppers with the denominators shown below. There are small tick marks on some of the number lines to help you divide the lines into equal parts. You will need to use a pencil and a ruler to complete the others.

The number line for thirds has been done as an example. Make the tick marks slightly larger for each fraction you label.

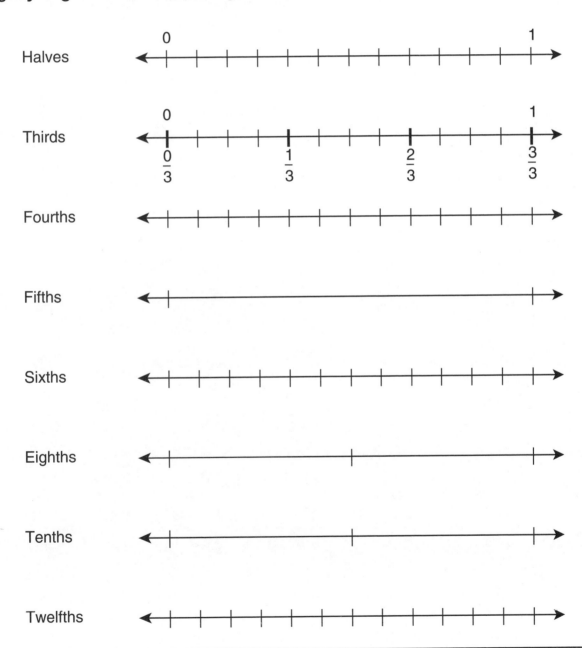

Unit 4

Division and Data

	Student Guide	Discovery Assignment Book	Adventure Book	Unit Resource Guide*
Lesson 1				
Grid Area	●	●		
Lesson 2				
Modeling Division	●			
Lesson 3				
Paper-and-Pencil Division	●			●
Lesson 4				
How Close Is Close Enough?	●	●		●
Lesson 5				
Mean or Median?	●			
Lesson 6				
Spreading Out	●			
Lesson 7				
George Washington Carver: Man of Measure		●	●	
Lesson 8				
Review Problems	●			
Lesson 9				
Midterm Test				●

Unit Resource Guide pages are from the teacher materials.

Unit 4 Home Practice

PART 1 *Triangle Flash Cards: Square Numbers*

Study for the quiz on the multiplication and division facts for the square numbers. Take home your *Triangle Flash Cards: Square Numbers* and your list of facts you need to study.

To quiz a multiplication fact, cover the corner containing the highest number. Multiply the two uncovered numbers.

To quiz a division fact, cover one of the smaller numbers. Use the two uncovered numbers to solve a division fact.

Mix up the multiplication and division facts. Sometimes cover the highest number and sometimes cover a smaller number.

Your teacher will tell you when the quiz on the square numbers will be given.

PART 2 Area

Solve the following problems. Choose an appropriate method for each: mental math, paper and pencil, or a calculator. Explain your solutions. Use a separate sheet of paper to show your work.

1. Jessie's parents are buying a rug for Jessie's bedroom. Jessie measured the length and width of her bedroom floor. It is 10 feet by 10 feet. What is the area of her bedroom floor?

2. Arti is putting together a jigsaw puzzle. The finished puzzle is 36 cm by 40 cm. What is the area of the puzzle?

3. Jerome's grandmother has an 8-inch by 10-inch wedding picture of herself and Jerome's grandfather. Her wedding picture sits next to Jerome's 3-inch by 5-inch school picture. About how many times greater in area is the wedding picture than the school picture?

4. A. Nila's older sister has a dog run for her dog in the backyard. The run is 12 feet by 8 feet. What is the area of the dog run?

   B. Nila wants to put the same size dog run in her backyard. If her backyard is 100 square feet, will an 8 feet by 12 feet dog run fit?

PART 3 Multiplication and Division Practice

Solve the following problems using a paper-and-pencil method. Estimate to be sure your answers are reasonable.

A. $49 \times 9 =$ **B.** $135 \div 6 =$ **C.** $18 \times 45 =$ **D.** $1064 \div 4 =$

E. $22 \times 76 =$ **F.** $2834 \div 3 =$ **G.** $8505 \div 7 =$ **H.** $1063 \times 3 =$

I. $1894 \times 4 =$ **J.** $7720 \div 8 =$ **K.** $2460 \times 6 =$ **L.** $8070 \div 5 =$

PART 4 Comparing Prices

While stocking shelves at her father's store, Arti compares the prices of two different brands of pencils. She showed the information in the following graphs. Use the graphs to answer the questions below. Use a separate sheet of paper for your explanations.

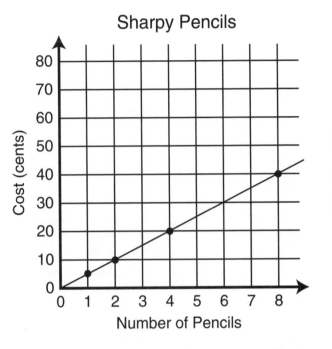

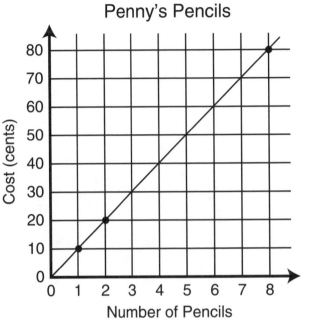

1. Write a ratio of cost to the number of pencils for Sharpy Pencils.

2. Write a ratio of cost to number of pencils for Penny's Pencils.

3. Which pencils are more expensive? How do you know?

4. Which line is steeper?

Show as many ways as you can to solve the following problems.

5. What is the cost of four Sharpy Pencils?

6. How many of Penny's Pencils can you buy with 60¢?

7. How many Sharpy Pencils can you buy with 60¢?

PART 5 Word Problems

**Solve the following problems. Choose an appropriate method for each:
mental math, paper and pencil, or a calculator. Explain your solutions.
Use a separate sheet of paper to show your work.**

1. Mighty Tree Tree Farm is having a sale. Seedlings (very young trees) are
   grouped in bunches of 15 for $25.00, tax included. Coleman School decided
   to buy 6 bunches to plant on the school grounds.

   A. How many seedlings did Coleman School buy?

   B. How much money did Coleman School spend?

2. Mr. Moreno's class volunteered to plant the seedlings on the school
   grounds. There are 22 students present in Mr. Moreno's class on planting
   day. If each student plants about the same number of seedlings, how many
   seedlings will each student plant?

3. Mighty Tree Tree Farm also sells older trees. They charge $8.00 per foot in
   height for older trees, tax included. Jacob's family chooses to buy two trees
   that are the same height. The total cost is $128. How tall are the two trees?

4. Once a year, Mighty Tree Tree Farm has a Truckload Bargain Day. On this
   day, customers pay $250 and get a truckload of trees. One truckload has
   9 trees. Estimate the cost of one tree in this truckload.

5. This year, Mighty Tree Tree Farm sold 32 truckloads at $250 each.
   How much money did Mighty Tree Tree Farm take in on this day?

6. Last year, Mighty Tree Tree Farm sold 450 trees on Truckload Bargain Day.
   If each truckload contained 9 trees, how many truckloads did they sell?

7. Alexis is at the tree farm with her sister and her father. They wish to
   purchase a tree to plant in their backyard. They like five different kinds
   of trees. The heights of the trees they like are: 3 feet, 4 feet, 5 feet, 2 feet,
   and 6 feet.

   A. If they choose the tree with the median height, which tree would
      they choose?

   B. What is the mean height of the five trees they like?

Triangle Flash Cards: Square Numbers

- Work with a partner. Each partner cuts out the flash cards below.
- Your partner chooses one card at a time and covers one corner.
- To quiz you on a multiplication fact, your partner covers the shaded number. Multiply the two uncovered numbers.
- To quiz you on a division fact, your partner covers one of the smaller numbers on each card. Solve a division fact with the two uncovered numbers.
- Divide the cards into three piles: those facts you know and can answer quickly, those you can figure out with a strategy, and those you need to learn.
- Practice the last two piles again. Then make a list of the facts you need to practice at home.
- Repeat the directions for your partner.

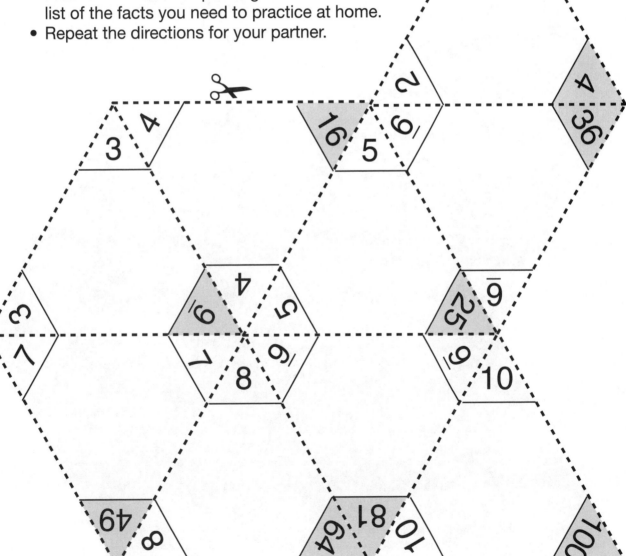

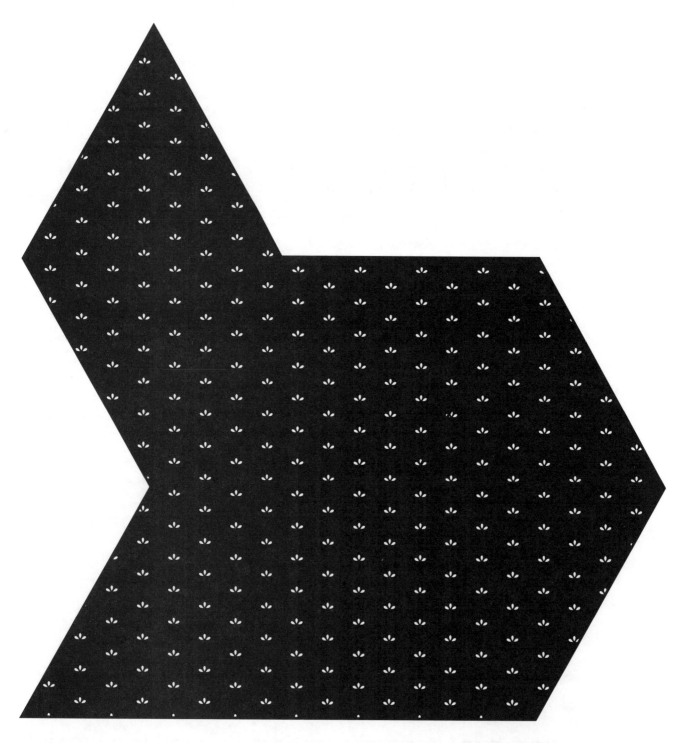

Name _____ Date _____

Strategies to Find Area

Use two methods to find the area of each shape. Share your strategies.

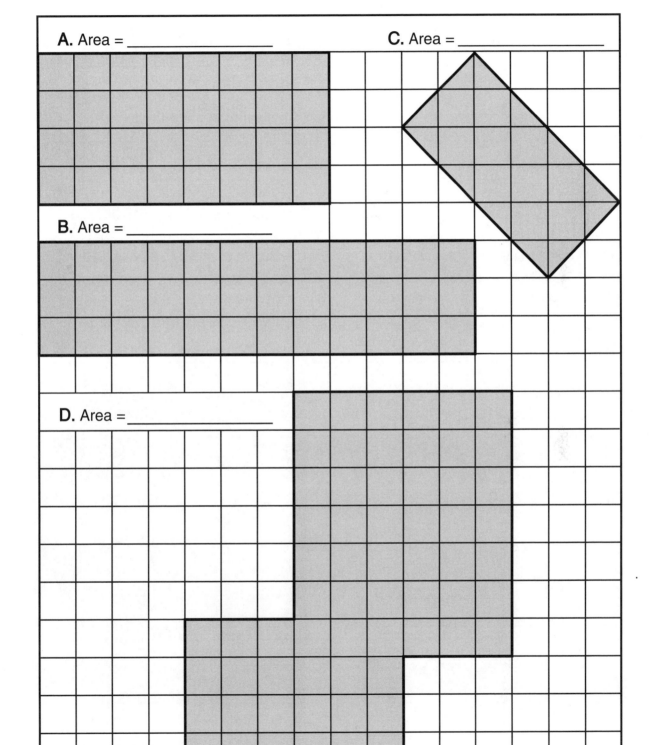

A. Area = _____

C. Area = _____

B. Area = _____

D. Area = _____

Name _____   Date _____

Look at the two shapes below. Find the area of each using two different methods. What can you say about the two shapes?

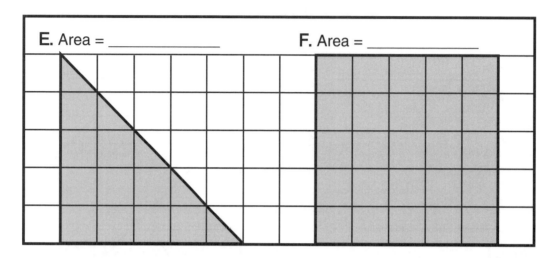

E. Area = _____   **F.** Area = _____

Sometimes you will need to find the area of a shape that has curved sides. Look at the shapes below. Estimate the area of these shapes. Then describe your strategy.

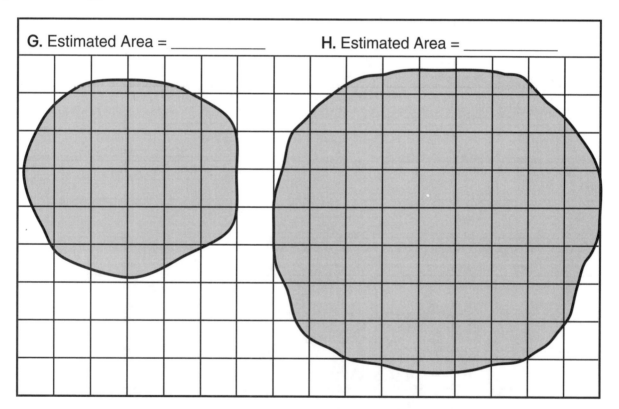

G. Estimated Area = _____   **H.** Estimated Area = _____

Compare your estimated areas of Shapes G and H to your classmates' estimates. Find the median of the estimated areas for Shape G. Find the median of the estimated areas for Shape H.

Name _____ Date _____

Finding Area

Find the area of each shape. Then on a separate sheet of paper, explain how you found the area. You may wish to use number sentences in your explanations.

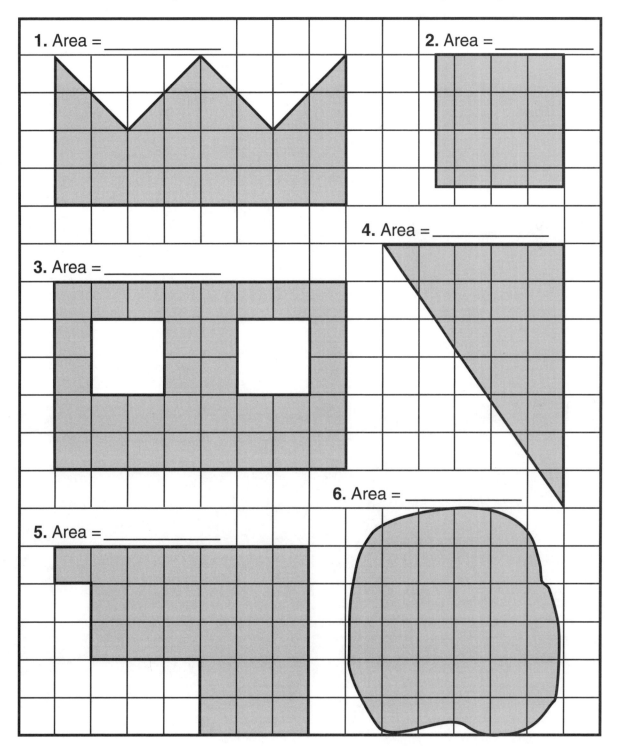

1. Area = _____

2. Area = _____

3. Area = _____

4. Area = _____

5. Area = _____

6. Area = _____

Name _____ Date _____

Under the Rug

What strategies could be used to find the area of the shaded rectangle in Figure C and the shape in Figure D?

Figure C

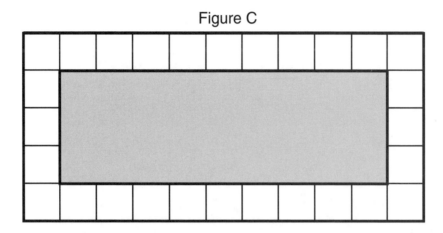

Figure D

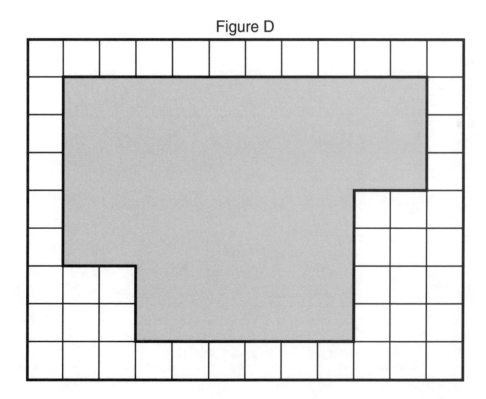

Cut and Paste Puzzles

1. Think about everything that you know about area. Does the area of a shape change if it is cut into pieces and pasted back together into a different shape? Look at the three shapes on the next page. Find the area of each. Do not measure with a ruler.

   A. Area of A = _____

   B. Area of B = _____

   C. Area of C = _____

2. Do you think that you can cut Shape B into pieces and paste it so it exactly

   covers Shape A? _____

   Explain your thinking. _____

   _____

   If you answered yes, then try it. Did it work? _____

3. Do you think you can cut apart Shape A and paste it so that it exactly

   covers Shape B? _____

   Explain your thinking. _____

   _____

   If you answered yes, then try it. Did it work? _____

4. Do you think you can cut apart Shape C and paste it so that it exactly

   covers Shape A? _____

   Explain your thinking. _____

   _____

   _____

   If you answered yes, then try it. Did it work? _____

Use these figures for your cut and paste puzzles:

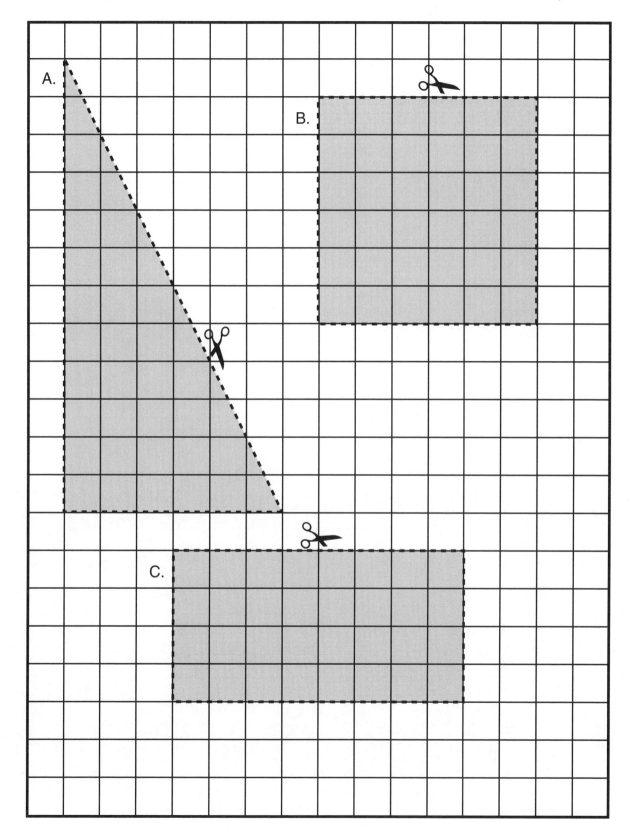

Here is an extra set of shapes.

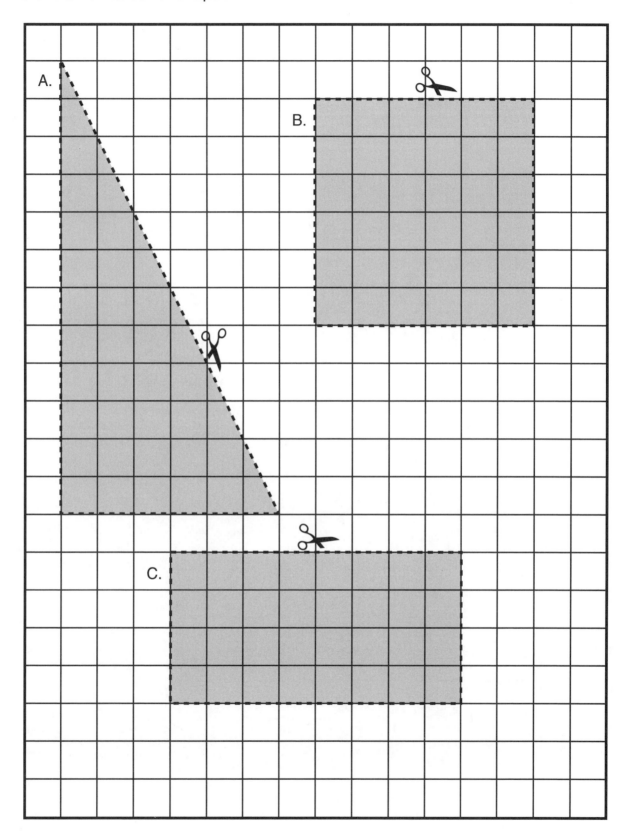

Super Challenge: Cut and Paste Puzzle

1. Challenge: Find the area of Shape A below and Shape B on the following page. Do not measure with a ruler.

   A. Shape A = _____

   B. Shape B = _____

2. Can you cut apart Shape A to cover Shape B exactly? _____

   Explain. _____

   _____

   If so, cut Shape A into as few pieces as possible and paste them to cover Shape B.

Shape A

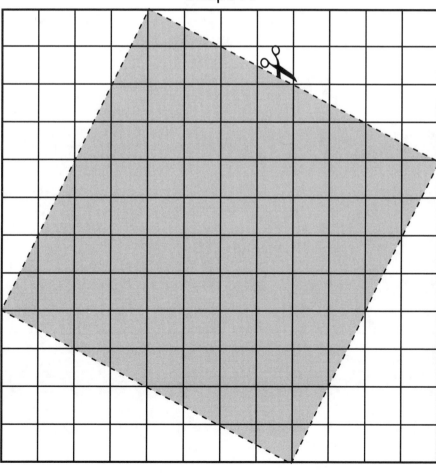

Shape B

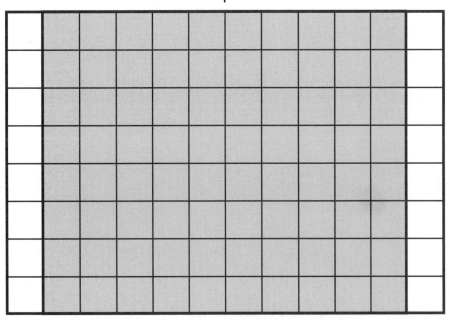

Shape A

A second copy of Shape A is here if you need to start over.

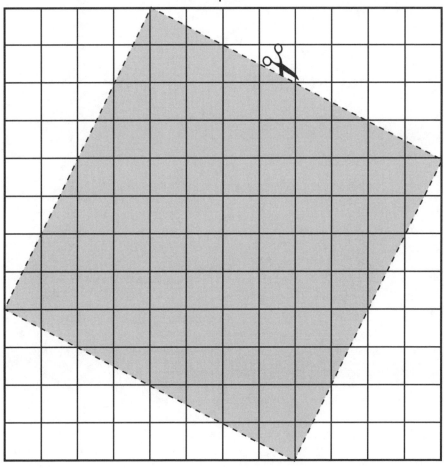

10% Chart

Your group has been assigned one of seven shapes to measure. Make sure everyone in your group has estimated the area of the shape and has recorded his or her data in a table. Then make sure your group has found the median estimate for the area. Fill in the first two columns of the data table below with the results from your group and the other six groups. Your teacher will discuss the last three columns.

Shape	*M* Median Estimate	*M* ÷ 10 (Calculated)	10% of the Median (Estimated)	Range

Variables

1. In *George Washington Carver: Man of Measure*, Professor Carver names five variables often used in math and science. Use these variables and Carver's discussion to fill in the table below.

Variable	Common Use (Example where the variable is used)	Standard Units	Equipment Needed for Measurement

2. Think of another variable that could be added to Professor Carver's list and add it to the data table.

Unit 5

Investigating Fractions

	Student Guide	Discovery Assignment Book	Adventure Book	Unit Resource Guide*
Lesson 1				
Geoboard Fractions	●			
Lesson 2				
Parts and Wholes	●			
Lesson 3				
Using Dot Paper Rectangles	●	●		
Lesson 4				
Using Common Denominators	●			
Lesson 5				
A Day at the Races	●			
Lesson 6				
Adding Fractions with Rectangles	●			
Lesson 7				
Adding and Subtracting Fractions	●			●
Lesson 8				
Shannon's Trip to School	●			

Unit Resource Guide pages are from the teacher materials.

Unit 5 Home Practice

PART 1 *Triangle Flash Cards: 9s*

Study for the quiz on the multiplication and division facts for the nines. Take home your *Triangle Flash Cards: 9s* and your list of facts you need to study.

Ask a family member to choose one flash card at a time. To quiz you on a multiplication fact, he or she should cover the corner containing the highest number. Multiply the two uncovered numbers.

To quiz you on a division fact, your family member can cover one of the smaller numbers. One of the smaller numbers is circled. The other has a square around it. Use the two uncovered numbers to solve a division fact.

Ask your family member to mix up the multiplication and division facts. He or she should sometimes cover the highest number, sometimes cover the circled number, and sometimes cover the number in the square.

Your teacher will tell you when the quiz on the 9s will be given.

PART 2 Order of Operations

Solve the following problems using the order of operations.

A. $33 - 8 \times 3 =$

B. $35 \div 7 - 3 =$

C. $150 + 9 \times 6 =$

D. $45 \div 9 \times 4 =$

E. $100 + 200 \div 10 =$

F. $(6 + 3) \times 100 =$

G. $200 - (2 \times 70) =$

H. $60 \times 60 \div 40 =$

I. $(80 + 80) \div 40 =$

PART 3 Ratios

Leo made this graph. It shows the number of blocks and their total length in centimeters.

Use the graph to answer the following questions. Explain or show how you solved each problem. If you find more than one way to solve the problem, describe each method.

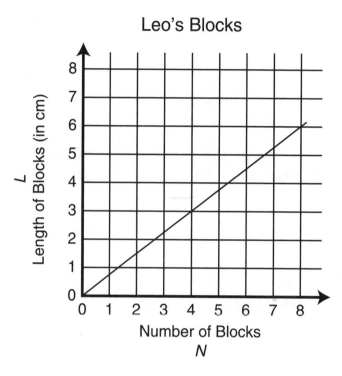

Leo's Blocks

1. Write the ratio of length to the number of blocks as a fraction.

2. Find the length of four blocks.

3. How many blocks will measure six centimeters?

4. Find the length of 40 blocks.

5. Find the length of 60 blocks.

Name _____ Date _____

PART 4 Fractions

You will need *Centimeter Dot Paper* to complete this part.

1. Complete each number sentence. Draw a picture on dot paper for each fraction. A 3 × 4 rectangle is one whole.

   A. $1\frac{2}{3} = \frac{n}{3}$

   B. $2\frac{3}{4} = \frac{n}{4}$

   C. $1\frac{1}{6} = \frac{n}{6}$

   D. $3\frac{1}{6} = \frac{n}{6}$

2. Write each mixed number as an improper fraction.

   A. $2\frac{3}{5} =$ _____

   B. $3\frac{1}{4} =$ _____

   C. $3\frac{3}{10} =$ _____

   D. $3\frac{5}{8} =$ _____

3. Write each improper fraction as a mixed number.

   A. $\frac{13}{6} =$ _____

   B. $\frac{7}{2} =$ _____

   C. $\frac{10}{3} =$ _____

   D. $\frac{14}{5} =$ _____

PART 5 Practicing the Operations

1. Solve the following problems in your head. Estimate the answers to F and G.

   A. 240 + 60 = _____

   B. 2089 + 401 = _____

   C. 1250 − 300 = _____

   D. 10,000 − 6700 = _____

   E. 3800 + 1200 = _____

   F. Estimate: 89 × 18

   G. Estimate: 1270 ÷ 50

2. Use a separate sheet of paper. Solve the following problems using a paper-and-pencil method. Estimate to be sure your answers are reasonable.

   A. 473 + 1548 = _____

   B. 28 × 59 = _____

   C. 7034 ÷ 9 = _____

   D. 3704 − 478 = _____

PART 6 More Work with Fractions

You will need two pieces of dot paper to complete Questions 2 and 3 of this part.

1. Write three equivalent fractions for each of the following fractions.

   A. $\frac{4}{10}$ = _____ = _____ = _____   B. $\frac{2}{3}$ = _____ = _____ = _____

2. Add $\frac{1}{2}$ to each of the following fractions using dot paper rectangles. Label each rectangle.

   A. $\frac{1}{2}$ B. $\frac{1}{3}$ C. $\frac{3}{8}$ D. $\frac{5}{6}$

3. Subtract $\frac{1}{4}$ from each of the following fractions using dot paper rectangles.

   A. $\frac{3}{4}$ B. $\frac{7}{8}$ C. $\frac{1}{3}$ D. $\frac{11}{12}$

4. Write three fractions that are between $\frac{1}{4}$ and $\frac{1}{2}$. _____, _____, _____

5. Write four fractions that are less than $\frac{1}{4}$. _____, _____, _____, _____

PART 7 Solving Problems

Solve the following problems. Choose an appropriate method for each: mental math, paper and pencil, or a calculator. Explain your solutions. Use a separate sheet of paper to show your work.

1. The Yum Yum Deli makes sandwich trays for parties.

   A. Twenty-four sandwiches come on a large tray. If a company orders 27 trays for a party, how many sandwiches are they ordering?

   B. There will be 527 people attending the company party. Can each person have more than one sandwich? Explain.

2. Sturdy paper plates come in packages of 8. How many packages of plates should the Yum Yum Deli supply so that each of the 527 people can have one plate?

3. Of the guests attending, about $\frac{7}{12}$ are working employees. $\frac{1}{6}$ are retired employees. The rest are family members. What fraction of the guests are not employees?

Triangle Flash Cards: 9s

- Work with a partner. Each partner cuts out the flash cards below.
- Your partner chooses one card at a time and covers one corner.
- To quiz you on a multiplication fact, your partner covers the shaded number. Multiply the two uncovered numbers.
- To quiz you on a division fact, your partner covers the number in the square or the number in the circle. Solve a division fact with the two uncovered numbers.
- Divide the cards into three piles: those facts you know and can answer quickly, those you can figure out with a strategy, and those you need to learn.
- Practice the last two piles again. Then make a list of the facts you need to practice at home.
- Repeat the directions for your partner.

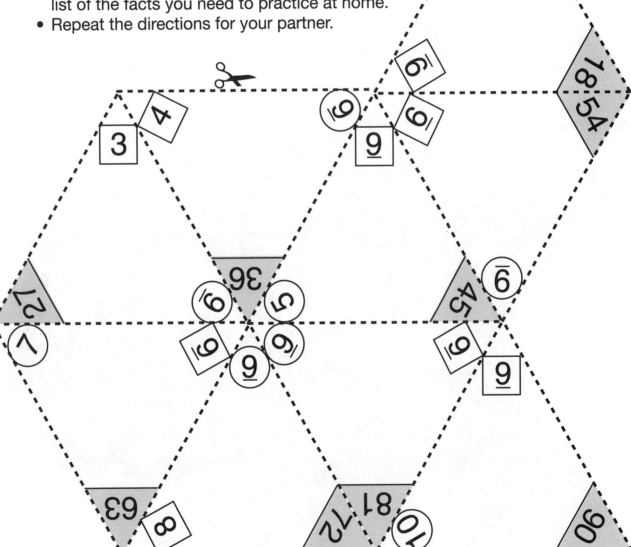

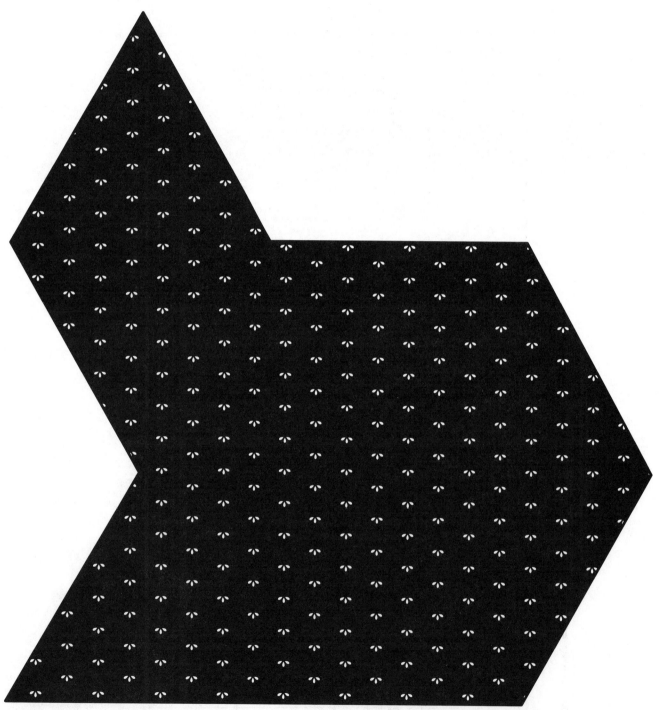

Equivalent Fractions on Dot Paper

The rectangle outlined in bold is one whole. Follow the directions beneath each rectangle to show equivalent fractions as in the example.

Example:

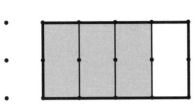 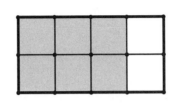

Change to eighths.

$\frac{3}{4} = \frac{\square}{8}$ $\frac{3}{4} = \frac{6}{8}$

I. A.   **B.**   **C.**

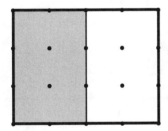   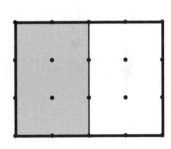

Change to fourths.   Change to sixths.   Change to twelfths.

$\frac{1}{2} = \frac{\square}{4}$ $\frac{1}{2} = \frac{\square}{6}$ $\frac{1}{2} = \frac{\square}{12}$

Name _____   Date _____

2. **A.**

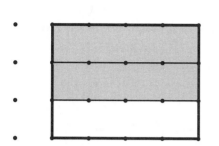

Change to sixths.

$$\frac{2}{3} = \frac{\boxed{}}{6}$$

B.

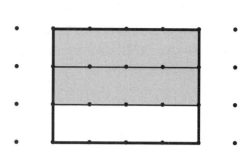

Change to twelfths.

$$\frac{2}{3} = \frac{\boxed{}}{12}$$

3. **A.**

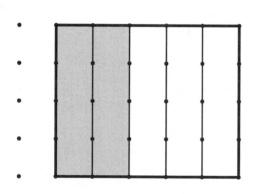

Change to tenths.

$$\frac{2}{5} = \frac{\boxed{}}{10}$$

B.

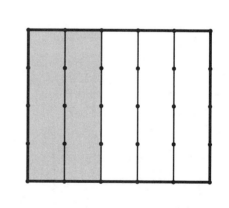

Change to twentieths.

$$\frac{2}{5} = \frac{\boxed{}}{20}$$

4. Complete the following number sentences.

A. $\frac{1}{4} = \frac{n}{16}$ B. $\frac{2}{3} = \frac{n}{9}$ C. $\frac{1}{2} = \frac{5}{n}$

D. $\frac{8}{16} = \frac{n}{4}$ E. $\frac{5}{3} = \frac{n}{6}$ F. $\frac{1}{4} = \frac{n}{100}$

G. $\frac{3}{15} = \frac{1}{n}$ H. $\frac{3}{4} = \frac{n}{12}$ I. $\frac{7}{12} = \frac{n}{24}$

Unit 6

Geometry

	Student Guide	Discovery Assignment Book	Adventure Book	Unit Resource Guide*
Lesson 1				
Angle Measures	●	●		
Lesson 2				
Angles in Triangles and Other Polygons	●	●		
Lesson 3				
Polygon Angles	●	●		
Lesson 4				
Congruent Shapes	●			
Lesson 5				
Quilts and Tessellations	●			
Lesson 6				
Classifying Shapes	●	●		
Lesson 7				
Making Shapes	●			●

Unit Resource Guide pages are from the teacher materials.

Unit 6 Home Practice

PART 1 *Triangle Flash Cards: Last Six Facts*

Study for the quiz on the multiplication and division facts for the last six facts $(4 \times 6, 4 \times 7, 4 \times 8, 6 \times 7, 6 \times 8,$ and $7 \times 8)$. Take home your *Triangle Flash Cards: Last Six Facts* and your list of facts you need to study.

Ask a family member to choose one flash card at a time. To quiz you on a multiplication fact, he or she should cover the corner containing the highest number. Multiply the two uncovered numbers.

To quiz you on a division fact, your family member can cover one of the smaller numbers. One of the smaller numbers is circled. The other has a square around it. Use the two uncovered numbers to solve a division fact.

Ask your family member to mix up the multiplication and division facts. He or she should sometimes cover the highest number, sometimes cover the circled number, and sometimes cover the number in the square.

Your teacher will tell you when the quiz on the last six facts will be given.

PART 2 **Practicing Addition and Subtraction**

Use paper and pencil to solve the following problems. Estimate to be sure your answers are reasonable. Use a separate sheet of paper, if you need more work space.

   A. $549 + 82 =$ _____   **B.** $629 - 347 =$ _____   **C.** $843 + 178 =$ _____

   D. $213 - 58 =$ _____   **E.** $7542 + 282 =$ _____   **F.** $1067 + 93 =$ _____

   G. $4057 - 492 =$ _____   **H.** $2715 + 206 =$ _____   **I.** $462 - 379 =$ _____

Name _____ Date _____

PART 3 Angles and Triangles

You will need a protractor to complete this section. Use the straight edge on your protractor to draw the angles and triangle in Questions 1, 2, and 4.

1. On a separate sheet of paper, draw an angle that is greater than 90°. Name the angle YTV. Then measure the angle to the nearest degree.

2. On a separate sheet of paper, draw an angle that is less than 45°. Name the angle RGM. Then measure the angle to the nearest degree.

3. If triangle ADK has two angles that are 40° each, what is the measure of the third angle? How do you know?

4. Can a triangle have two 70° angles and one that measures 50°? How do you know?

5. One angle in triangle QFP is a right angle. A second angle is 27°. What is the measure of the third angle? How do you know?

6. One angle in a triangle measures 32°. Another angle is twice as large. What is the measure of the third angle? How do you know?

PART 4 Practicing Multiplication and Division

Use paper and pencil to solve the following problems. Estimate to be sure your answers are reasonable. Use a separate sheet of paper to show your work.

A. $607 \times 8 =$ _____   B. $174 \times 9 =$ _____   C. $435 \div 3 =$ _____

D. $420 \div 9 =$ _____   E. $4631 \times 5 =$ _____   F. $768 \div 5 =$ _____

G. $68 \times 34 =$ _____   H. $577 \div 7 =$ _____   I. $1652 \div 4 =$ _____

GEOMETRY

PART 5 Slab-Maker Problems

Draw these shapes and answer the questions on a separate sheet of paper. You will need a centimeter ruler and a protractor.

1. Draw triangle DEF. The length of side EF is 5 cm. Angle F is a right angle. The length of DF is 12 cm. What is the length of side DE?

2. Draw rectangle GHIJ. The length of GH is 8 cm. The length of HI is half the length of GH. What is the area of this rectangle?

3. Draw quadrilateral QRST. The length of ST is 6 cm. Angles S and T are both 60°. The lengths of sides RS and QT are 2 cm. Which two line segments are parallel?

4. Draw a pentagon with two right angles. Have one side measure 4 cm and one side measure 5 cm. Do you think everyone will draw congruent pentagons? How do you know?

PART 6 Fractions

1. Solve the following addition and subtraction problems.

   A. $\frac{1}{2} + \frac{5}{8} =$ _____ **B.** $\frac{2}{3} + \frac{1}{12} =$ _____

   C. $\frac{7}{12} - \frac{1}{2} =$ _____ **D.** $\frac{3}{5} - \frac{3}{10} =$ _____

2. Draw pictures to help you answer these questions. You may use dot paper to help you.

   A. One furlong is $\frac{1}{8}$ mile. How many furlongs equal one mile?

   B. A tablespoon is $\frac{1}{16}$ of a cup. How many tablespoons equal one cup?

   C. One foot is $\frac{1}{3}$ of a yard. How many feet equal one yard?

   D. Five minutes is $\frac{1}{12}$ of an hour. How many minutes equal $\frac{3}{12}$ of an hour?

   E. Gold that is pure is called 24 karat gold. If 1 out of 24 parts is pure, it is 1 karat gold. Gold that is 10 karat is $\frac{10}{24}$ or $\frac{5}{12}$ pure. Is 14 karat gold more or less than $\frac{1}{2}$ pure gold?

PART 7 Travel Time Problems

Choose an appropriate method to solve each of the following problems. For some questions you may need to find an exact answer, while for others you may only need an estimate. For each question, you may choose to use paper and pencil, mental math, or a calculator. Use a separate sheet of paper to show how you solved each problem.

1. John and his family are driving from Chicago, Illinois, to Phoenix, Arizona. His family plans to take 4 days to make this trip. Phoenix is 1776 miles from Chicago. About how many miles should they drive each of the four days if they want to drive about the same amount each day?

2. On the first day of the trip, John's family leaves home at 7:30 A.M. They drive for 4 hours before stopping to eat lunch. If they average 62 miles per hour, how far did they drive before stopping?

3. At the end of the second day of driving, John's family has traveled 957 miles and has spent $16\frac{1}{2}$ hours on the road. About how many miles per hour did they average so far on their trip?

4. One night John's family stops for pizza. They order a large pizza that is $\frac{1}{2}$ pepperoni and $\frac{1}{2}$ cheese. It is cut into 16 slices of the same size. If John eats one slice of pepperoni and one slice of cheese, what fraction of the pizza is this?

5. In Phoenix, John's family stays in a hotel for 7 nights. The hotel costs $97.00 per night including tax. What is the total bill for their 7-night stay?

6. When John's family arrives home, he calculates the number of gallons of gasoline they used during their trip to and from Phoenix. The car averages about 24 miles per gallon.

   A. How many gallons of gas did they use during the drive to and from Phoenix?

   B. If the average cost of gasoline is $1.57 per gallon, how much money did John's family spend on gasoline during the trip?

Triangle Flash Cards: Last Six Facts

- Work with a partner. Each partner cuts out the flash cards below.
- Your partner chooses one card at a time and covers one corner.
- To quiz you on a multiplication fact, your partner covers the shaded number. Multiply the two uncovered numbers.
- To quiz you on a division fact, your partner covers the number in the square or the number in the circle. Solve a division fact with the two uncovered numbers.
- Divide the cards into three piles: those facts you know and can answer quickly, those you can figure out with a strategy, and those you need to learn.
- Practice the last two piles again. Then make a list of the facts you need to practice at home.
- Repeat the directions for your partner.

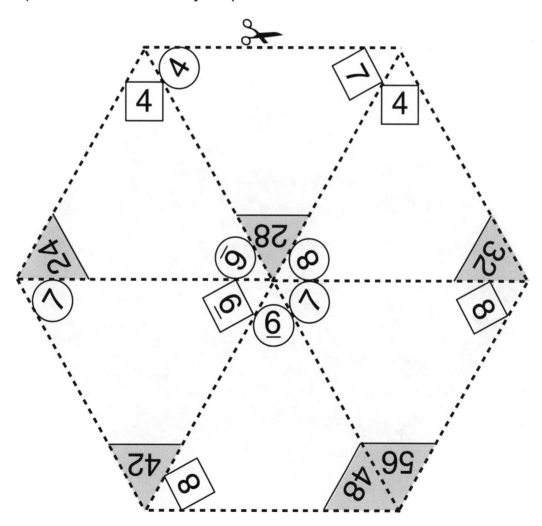

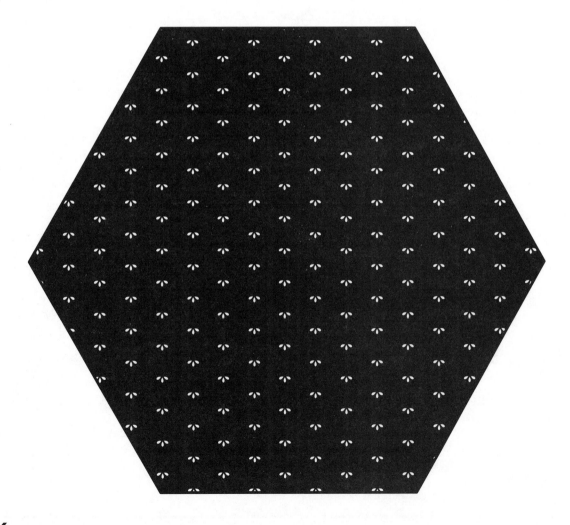

Measuring Angles

Measure each of the angles in Questions 1–8 with your protractor. You may need to extend the sides of some of the angles in order to measure.

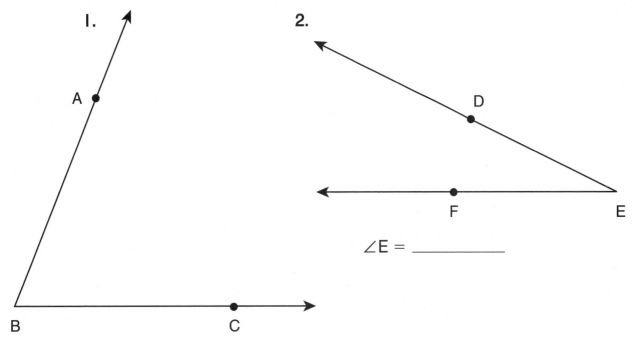

1.

2.

∠E = _____

∠B = _____

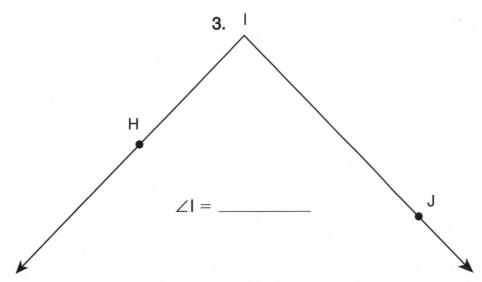

3.

∠I = _____

4.

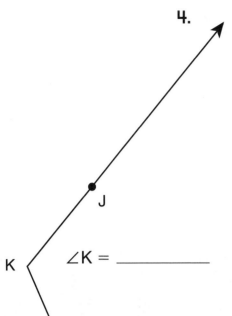

∠K = _____

5.

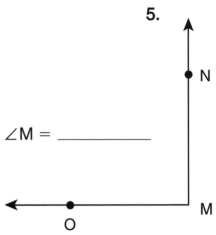

∠M = _____

6.

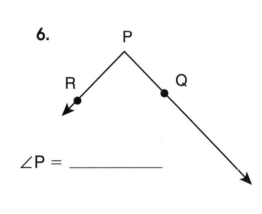

∠P = _____

7.

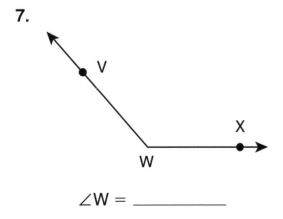

∠W = _____

8.

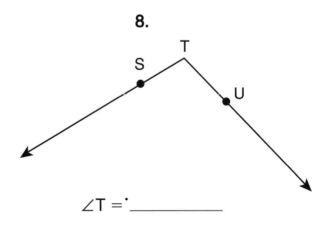

∠T = · _____

Measuring Pattern Block Angles

The 8 pattern blocks are pictured and named. All of these shapes are polygons.

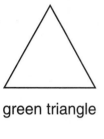

green triangle

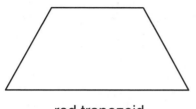

red trapezoid

square

purple triangle

tan rhombus

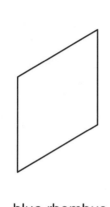

blue rhombus

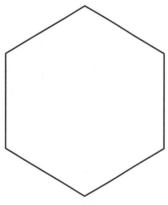

hexagon

brown trapezoid

1. Find the measures of the angles of the green triangle. Write the angle measures inside the pictured triangle. You may need to extend the sides.

2. Place 6 green triangles on top of the hexagon as pictured here. What is the degree measure of each of the angles of the hexagon? (*Hint:* You do not have to measure.) Write the angle measures inside the hexagon.

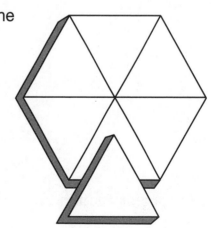

3. Find the angle measures for all the pattern blocks. You can use shortcuts to find angle measures.

4. Explain what shortcuts you can use to find the angle measures of the blue rhombus.

5. Explain what shortcuts you can use to find the angle measures of the red trapezoid.

6. Which of the pattern blocks are quadrilaterals?

A polygon whose sides all have equal length and whose angles all have the same degree measure is called a **regular** polygon.

7. When you lay the pattern blocks flat, the top surfaces are polygons. Which of the pattern blocks have tops that are regular polygons? Explain why.

8. Professor Peabody accidentally erased part of quadrilateral ABCD. All that is left is side BC, the bottom of the quadrilateral. See if you can redraw the quadrilateral using the following clues.

   Clues:
   - The measure of ∠B is 90 degrees.
   - Side AB is 4 cm long.
   - The measure of ∠C is 120 degrees.
   - Side CD is 6 cm long.

B   C

You should have enough information now to finish drawing quadrilateral ABCD.

9. ∠A = _____   10. ∠D = _____

11. AD = _____ cm

Angles in Triangles and Other Polygons

Polygon Angles Data Table

Fill in the rows for the triangle, quadrilateral, and pentagon. Leave the last column blank. Then complete the table through the dodecagon (12-sided polygon). Your class will discuss the entries for the final column and last row.

Polygon	Number of Sides	Number of Angles	Number of Triangles	Sum of Angles (degrees)	Measure of One Angle of a Regular Polygon (degrees)
triangle					
quadrilateral					
pentagon					
hexagon					
septagon					
octagon					
nonagon					
decagon					
11-gon					
dodecagon					
N-gon					

Shapes Zoo Pieces

Cut out the shapes and create a shapes zoo.

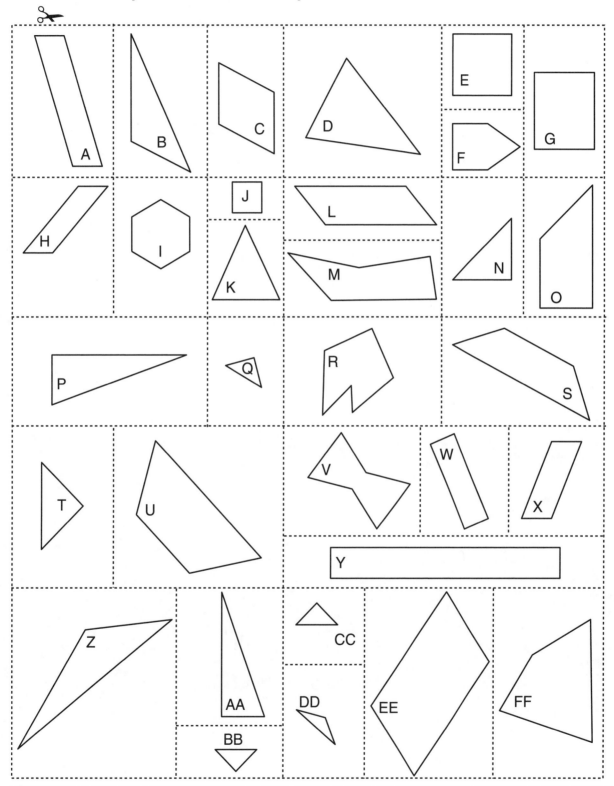

Unit 7

Decimals and Probability

	Student Guide	Discovery Assignment Book	Adventure Book	Unit Resource Guide*
Lesson 1				
Fractions, Decimals, and Percents	●	●		●
Lesson 2				
Decimal Models	●	●		●
Lesson 3				
Comparing and Rounding Decimals	●	●		
Lesson 4				
Adding and Subtracting Decimals	●	●		
Lesson 5				
Multiplying Decimals with Area	●			
Lesson 6				
Paper-and-Pencil Decimal Multiplication	●			●
Lesson 7				
Flipping One Coin	●			
Lesson 8				
Flipping Two Coins	●	●		
Lesson 9				
Families with Two Children	●			
Lesson 10				
Unlikely Heroes			●	

*Unit Resource Guide pages are from the teacher materials.

(Unit 7) Home Practice

PART 1 *Triangle Flash Cards: All the Facts*

Look at your *Multiplication* and *Division Facts I Know* charts. Take home your *Triangle Flash Cards* for all the facts you have not circled. With the help of a family member, use the cards to study a small group of facts (8 to 10 facts) each night.

Ask a family member to choose one flash card at a time. To quiz you on a multiplication fact, he or she should cover the corner containing the highest number. Multiply the two uncovered numbers.

To quiz you on a division fact, your family member can cover one of the smaller numbers. (One of the smaller numbers is circled. The other has a square around it.) Use the two uncovered numbers to solve a division fact.

Ask your family member to mix up the multiplication and division facts. He or she should sometimes cover the highest number, sometimes cover the circled number, and sometimes cover the number in the square.

PART 2 **Practicing the Operations**

Solve the following problems using paper and pencil. Estimate to be sure your answers are reasonable.

A. $248 + 275 =$ **B.** $8208 - 775 =$ **C.** $26 \times 54 =$

D. $893 \times 5 =$ **E.** $9 \overline{)11{,}346}$ **F.** $3 \overline{)1748}$

PART 3 Fractions, Decimals, and Percents

Fill in the chart, writing each number as a fraction, a decimal, and a percent.
The first one is done for you. Use your centiwheel if you need to.

	Fraction	Decimal	Percent		Fraction	Decimal	Percent
A.	$\frac{1}{4}$	.25	25%	F.	$\frac{20}{100}$		
B.		.98		G.		1.00	
C.	$\frac{5}{100}$			H.	$\frac{1}{100}$		
D.			16%	I.			75%
E.		.50		J.			7%

PART 4 Adding Fractions

Solve the following problems.

A. $\frac{1}{2} + \frac{1}{4} =$

B. $\frac{1}{2} + \frac{3}{4} =$

C. $\frac{1}{2} + \frac{1}{3} =$

D. $\frac{1}{2} + \frac{2}{3} =$

E. $\frac{1}{3} + \frac{1}{4} =$

F. $\frac{2}{3} + \frac{3}{4} =$

PART 5 Reading, Writing, and Ordering Decimals

Write the following numbers as decimals and then put them in order from
smallest to largest.

A. thirty-seven thousandths _____

B. two hundred forty-two and four-hundredths _____

C. one hundred nine and fourteen-thousandths _____

D. six hundred sixteen-thousandths _____

DECIMALS AND PROBABILITY

PART 6 Working with Decimals

Solve the following problems using paper and pencil. Estimate to be sure your answers are reasonable.

A. $45.6 + 12.35 =$ **B.** $0.76 + 0.043 =$ **C.** $0.89 \times 4 =$

D. $7.3 - 0.53 =$ **E.** $4.8 \times 8.3 =$ **F.** $0.67 \times 2 =$

G. $176.4 + 0.385 =$ **H.** $456.07 - 128.43 =$ **I.** $4.577 \times 0.5 =$

PART 7 What's the Chance?

Manny works at the miniature golf range. The owner bought 20 new balls. He bought 5 red balls, 2 white balls, 3 green balls, 7 orange balls, and 3 yellow balls. Manny put all the new balls in a bucket. In between customers, he tries a probability experiment. If Manny picks one ball, the probability that he will pick a yellow ball is $\frac{3}{20}$.

1. Without looking, he picks one ball from the bucket. Write each of the following probabilities as a fraction, decimal, and percent:
   A. The probability that he will pick a red ball.
   B. The probability that he will pick a white ball.
   C. The probability that he will pick a green ball.
   D. The probability that he will pick an orange ball.

2. What color ball will Manny most likely pick? Justify your answer.

3. Manny predicts that he will choose a red ball or an orange ball. Is this a good prediction? Why or why not?

PART 8 The Swim Meet

Choose an appropriate method to solve each of the following problems. For some questions you may need to find an exact answer, while for others you may only need an estimate. For each question, you may choose to use paper and pencil, mental math, or a calculator. Use a separate sheet of paper to explain how you solved each problem.

1. Shannon is on the swim team. She swam the backstroke in 7 meets. Her times for each race were 53.19 seconds, 49.67 seconds, 47.30 seconds, 43.86 seconds, 46.07 seconds, 45.87 seconds, and 45.91 seconds. What was Shannon's average speed for the backstroke during these meets? (Use the mean.)

2. A four-person team is needed to swim the medley relay. Each team member swims 50 meters using a different stroke. During one relay, Lin swam 50 meters using the butterfly stroke in 59.53 seconds, Shannon swam the backstroke in 46.12 seconds, Blanca swam the breaststroke in 53.27 seconds, and Grace finished with the freestyle stroke in 36.41 seconds.

   A. How many minutes and seconds did it take the team to complete the entire relay?

   B. What is the total distance that the relay team swam?

3. During the first swim meet of the season, Frank swam the 50-meter breaststroke event in 57.62 seconds. During the final meet of the season, he swam the 50-meter breaststroke in 44.51 seconds. How many seconds faster did Frank swim the 50-meter breaststroke at the end of the season than at the beginning?

4. During one swim meet Edward swam in 5 different events. He swam the 100-meter individual medley in 1 minute 38.30 seconds, the 50-meter butterfly in 42.48 seconds, the 50-meter breaststroke in 44.80 seconds, the 50-meter freestyle in 32.83 seconds, and the 50-meter backstroke in 45.87 seconds.

   A. How many meters did he swim during this meet?

   B. About how many minutes did Edward spend swimming during this meet?

5. The final swim meet of the season began at 8:30 A.M. It ended at 4:45 P.M. How long was the swim meet?

6. Parents held a bake sale during each meet to raise money for the team. During one meet, the parents sold cupcakes for $.25 each. They sold 42 cupcakes. How much money did they get for the cupcakes?

7. The ribbons for the winners cost $.08 each. During the swim season the team used 648 ribbons. About how much did the team spend on the ribbons for this season?

Name _____ Date _____

Designing Quilts

1. Design a quilt using this grid.
   - You must use all of these colors: blue, red, yellow, orange, and green.
   - You may use no more than 50 blue, 30 red, 25 yellow, 25 orange, and 9 green squares.

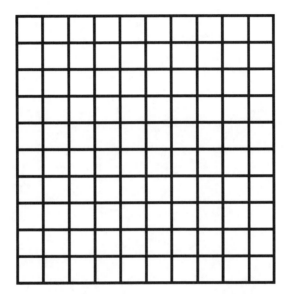

2. Complete the following data table for your quilt design.

Color	Number of Squares
Green	
Red	
Yellow	
Blue	
Orange	

Score One

Players

This game is played in pairs.

Materials

- two flat toothpicks
- decimal scale
- list of decimals prepared by each player

Rules

1. Each player makes a list of 20 decimals between 0–1 that have values in the hundredths. Example: 0.43, 0.19, 0.78, etc.

2. Cut out the decimal scale.

3. In turn, each player selects a decimal from his or her list and asks his or her partner to locate it on the number line. To earn .10 point, the partner estimates the position of the decimal on the number line and marks it with the toothpick within one-tenth of the actual location. The first player uses the decimal scale to verify the accuracy of the estimate.

4. The first person to accumulate one point is the winner.

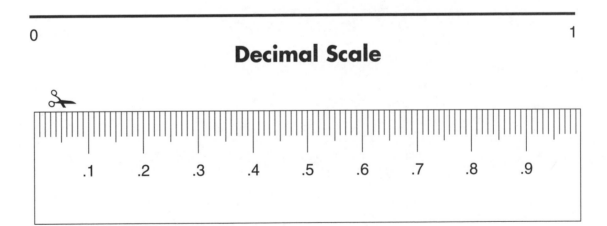

0   1

Decimal Scale

.1   .2   .3   .4   .5   .6   .7   .8   .9

Decimals: A Closer Look

1. **A.** Shade 0.86.

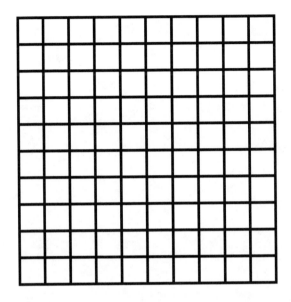

B. Write the decimal as a fraction. _____

C. Write the decimal as a percent. _____

D. Round 0.86 to the nearest tenth. _____

E. Is 0.86 closer to 0.1, 0.5, or 1? _____

2. **A.** Shade 0.462.

B. Write the decimal as a fraction.

_____

C. Round 0.462 to the nearest

hundredth. _____

D. Round 0.462 to the nearest tenth.

_____

E. Is 0.462 closer to 0.1, 0.5, or 1?

_____

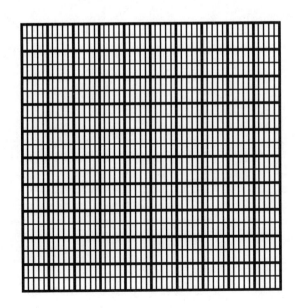

3. A. Shade $\frac{572}{1000}$.

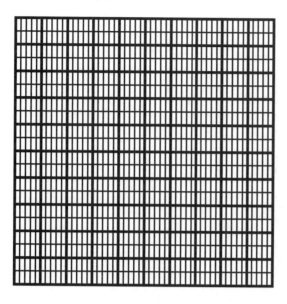

B. Write $\frac{572}{1000}$ as a decimal. _____

C. Round the decimal in Part B to the nearest hundredth. _____

D. Write the decimal in Part B as a percent (to the nearest percent).

_____

4. A. Shade $\frac{68}{1000}$.

B. Write $\frac{68}{1000}$ as a decimal.

_____

C. Round the decimal in Part B to the nearest hundredth.

_____

D. Write the decimal in Part B as a percent (to the nearest percent).

_____

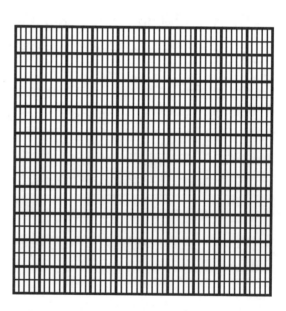

5. A. Shade 0.3.

B. Shade 0.30.

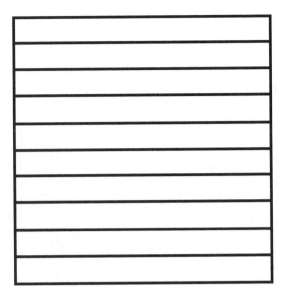

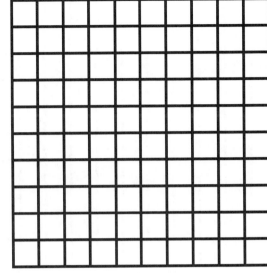

C. Write 0.3 as a fraction. _____

D. Write 0.30 as a fraction. _____

E. Write 0.3 as a percent. _____

F. Write 0.30 as a percent. _____

G. Is $\frac{3}{10} = \frac{30}{100}$? Explain how you know.

H. Write $<$, $>$, or $=$ in the box to make a true number sentence: 0.3 0.30

6. A. Shade 0.300.

B. Use $<$, $>$, or $=$ to make a true number sentence:

0.3 ☐ 0.300

C. Use $<$, $>$, or $=$ to make a true number sentence:

0.30 ☐ 0.300

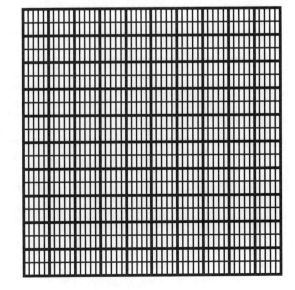

7. A. Shade 0.27.

B. Shade 0.127.

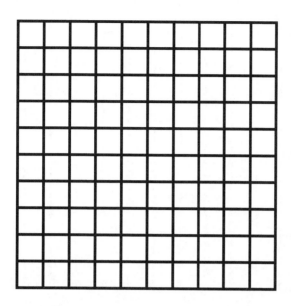

C. Use <, >, or = to make the number sentence true: 0.27 ☐ 0.127

8. A. Shade 0.4.

B. Shade 0.333.

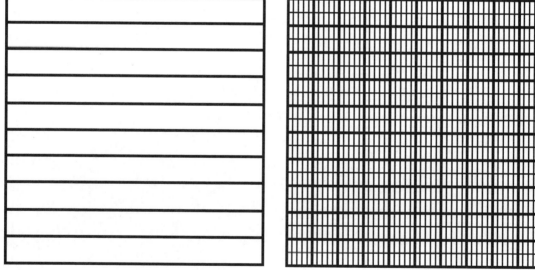

C. Use <, >, or = to make a true number sentence: 0.4 ☐ 0.333

Comparing and Rounding Decimals

9. **A.** Shade 1.83.

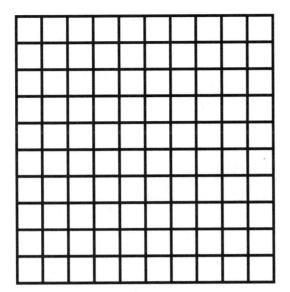 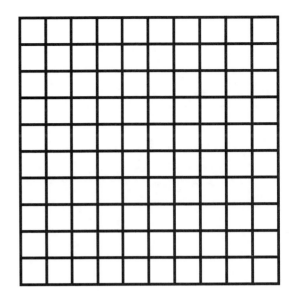

B. Write 1.83 as a mixed number. _____

C. Round 1.83 to the nearest tenth. _____

D. Round 1.83 to the nearest whole number. _____

10. **A.** Shade 1.27.

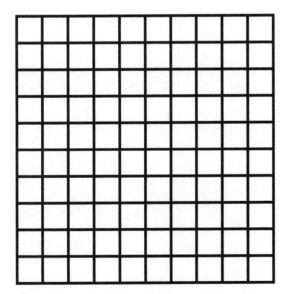 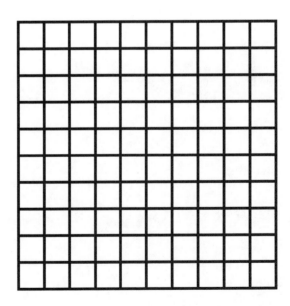

B. Write 1.27 as a mixed number. _____

C. Round 1.27 to the nearest tenth. _____

D. Round 1.27 to the nearest whole number. _____

Connect the Dots

Use a pencil and a ruler to connect the decimals in order from smallest to largest. Begin at 0.001 at the star. End at 1.0. Follow the dotted arrow to help you get started.

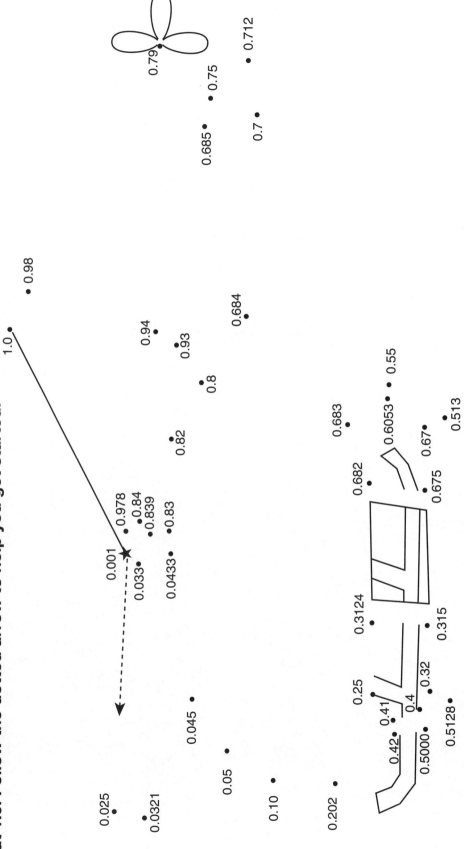

Adding Decimals with Grids

1. Irma is training for a bike race. Her coach wants her to ride at least one, but no more than two miles a day. She knows that it is 0.4 mile to the park. If she makes a round trip, will she meet her coach's requirements?

   A. Shade 0.4 of the grid.

   B. Shade another 0.4 of the grid.

   C. How far will Irma ride?

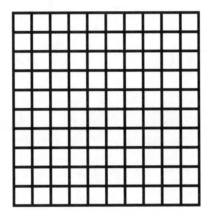

2. Lin walks 0.25 mile to the store and then 0.4 mile farther to her grandmother's house.

   A. Does Lin walk more or less than $\frac{1}{2}$ mile? More or less than 1 mile?

   B. How far does she walk in all? Use the grid to add.

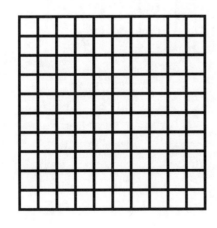

3. Roberto runs 0.8 mile to the ball field and then 0.6 mile around the field.

    A. Does Roberto run more or less than one mile?

    B. How far does he run in all? Use the grids to add.

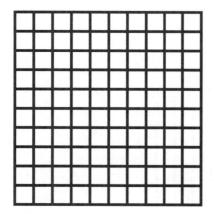 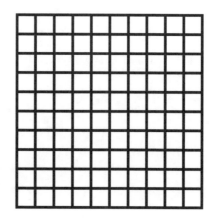

Use these grids to help solve the following addition problems.

    4. 0.6 + 0.26 = _____   **5.** 0.45 + 0.47 = _____

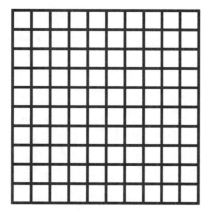 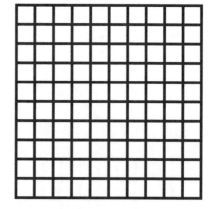

6. 0.67 + 1.09 = _____   (*Hint:* Use both grids.)

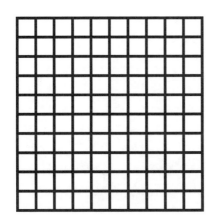 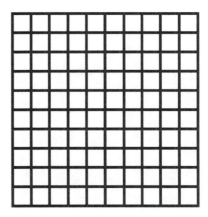

7. 0.3 + 0.87 = _____

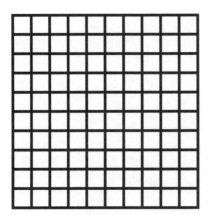 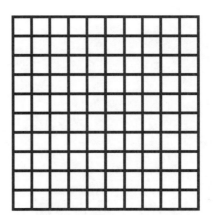

8. 1.47 + 0.03 = _____   Estimate to see if your answer is reasonable.

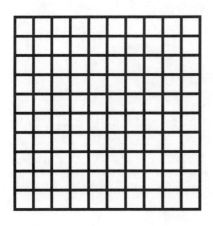 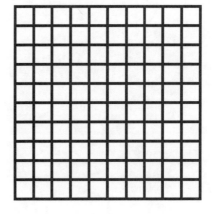

Subtracting Decimals with Grids

1. Blanca is building shelves. She has a board that is 0.85 m long. She cuts 0.2 m from the board.

   A. Use a pencil to lightly shade 0.85 of the grid.

   B. Erase 0.2 of the shaded part.

   C. How long is the board after she cuts it?

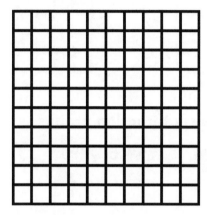

2. Edward and Romesh made paper airplanes and measured the distance they flew. Edward's airplane went 0.9 meter and Romesh's went 0.26 meter.

   A. Whose plane went farther?

   B. Use the grid to find out how much farther.

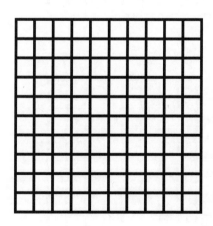

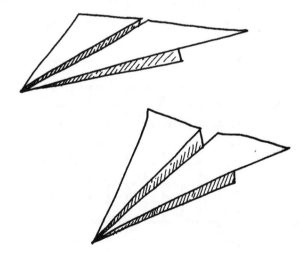

---

3. Jerome is 1.3 m tall. His little brother is 0.95 m tall. How much taller is Jerome? Use the grids to solve the problem.

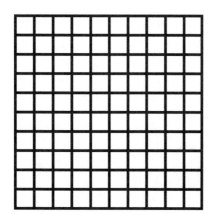   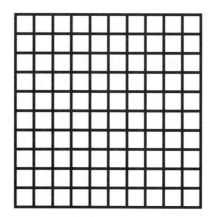

Use the grids to solve these subtraction problems.

4. 0.6 − 0.08 = _____   **5.** 0.95 − 0.7 = _____

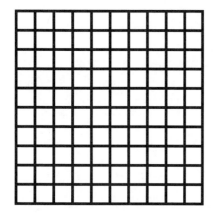   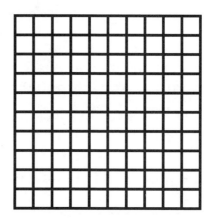

6. 0.28 − 0.09 = _____   **7.** 0.12 − 0.08 = _____

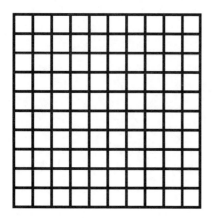   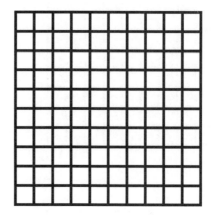

100 Two-Coin Flips

Trial	Outcome	Number of Heads	Trial	Outcome	Number of Heads	Trial	Outcome	Number of Heads	Trial	Outcome	Number of Heads
1.			26.			51.			76.		
2.			27.			52.			77.		
3.			28.			53.			78.		
4.			29.			54.			79.		
5.			30.			55.			80.		
6.			31.			56.			81.		
7.			32.			57.			82.		
8.			33.			58.			83.		
9.			34.			59.			84.		
10.			35.			60.			85.		
11.			36.			61.			86.		
12.			37.			62.			87.		
13.			38.			63.			88.		
14.			39.			64.			89.		
15.			40.			65.			90.		
16.			41.			66.			91.		
17.			42.			67.			92.		
18.			43.			68.			93.		
19.			44.			69.			94.		
20.			45.			70.			95.		
21.			46.			71.			96.		
22.			47.			72.			97.		
23.			48.			73.			98.		
24.			49.			74.			99.		
25.			50.			75.			100.		

Coin Flipping Data Tables

10-Trial Table

Number of Heads	*N* Number of Trials Out of 10	$\frac{N}{10}$ Fraction of Trials Out of 10	Equivalent Fraction with Denominator of 100	Percent of 10 Trials
0				
1				
2				

100-Trial Table

Number of Heads	Number of Trials Out of 100	Fraction of Trials Out of 100	Percent of 100 Trials
0			
1			
2			

1000-Trial Table

Number of Heads	Number of Trials for Each Group										Total Number of Trials Out of 1000	Fraction of Trials Out of 1000	Decimal	Nearest Hundredth	Nearest Percent
	Gr.1	Gr.2	Gr.3	Gr.4	Gr.5	Gr.6	Gr.7	Gr.8	Gr.9	Gr.10					
0															
1															
2															

Comparing Probability with Results

Probabilities of Coin Flipping

Number of Heads	Ways Heads Can Come Up	Probability (as a fraction)	Probability (as a percent)
0			
1			
2			

Results of Coin Flipping

Number of Heads	Percent of 10 Trials	Percent of 100 Trials	Percent of 1000 Trials
0			
1			
2			

Unit 8

Applications:
An Assessment Unit

	Student Guide	Discovery Assignment Book	Adventure Book	Unit Resource Guide*
Lesson 1				
Experiment Review	●	●		
Lesson 2				
Three in a Row		●		
Lesson 3				
Florence Kelley	●		●	
Lesson 4				
Florence Kelley's Report				●
Lesson 5				
Life Spans	●	●		
Lesson 6				
Comparing Lives of Animals and Soap Bubbles	●	●		
Lesson 7				
Review Problems	●			
Lesson 8				
Midyear Test				●
Lesson 9				
Portfolio Review	●			

Unit Resource Guide pages are from the teacher materials.

125

Unit 8 · Home Practice

PART 1 *Triangle Flash Cards: All the Facts*

Study for the test on the multiplication and division facts. Take home the flash cards for the facts you need to study.

Ask a family member to choose one flash card at a time. To quiz you on a multiplication fact, he or she should cover the corner containing the highest number. Multiply the two uncovered numbers.

To quiz you on a division fact, your family member can cover one of the smaller numbers. One of the smaller numbers is circled. The other has a square around it. Use the two uncovered numbers to solve a division fact.

Ask your family member to mix up the multiplication and division facts. He or she should sometimes cover the highest number, sometimes cover the circled number, and sometimes cover the number in the square.

Your teacher will tell you when the test on the facts will be given.

PART 2 **Practicing the Operations**

1. Use paper and pencil to solve the following problems. Estimate each answer to make sure it is reasonable. Show your work on a separate sheet of paper.

   A. $72 \times 61 =$ **B.** $0.43 + 7.6 =$ **C.** $3804 \div 7 =$ **D.** $61 \times 0.29 =$

2. Estimate the following answers. Describe your strategy for each.

   A. $78,000 \div 40$

   B. $104,000 \div 27$

   C. 9821×14

   D. $178 \times 324,000$

PART 3 Review of Fractions

1. Solve the following problems.

   A. $\frac{7}{8} + \frac{3}{4} =$ B. $\frac{5}{6} - \frac{1}{3} =$ C. $\frac{11}{12} - \frac{1}{4} =$

2. Change the following mixed numbers to fractions.

   A. $7\frac{1}{3}$ B. $3\frac{2}{5}$ C. $11\frac{1}{8}$

3. Change the following fractions to mixed numbers.

   A. $\frac{14}{3}$ B. $\frac{65}{7}$ C. $\frac{103}{10}$

PART 4 Geometry Review

1. Find the area of the shape at the right.

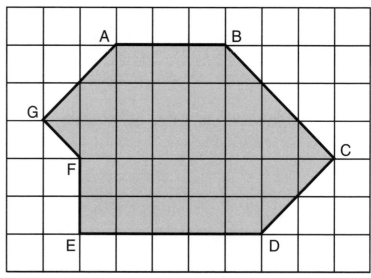

2. What is the measure of $\angle$C? You may use a protractor.

3. What is the measure of $\angle$D? You may use a protractor.

4. A rectangle measures 5.5 cm by 4.6 cm. Is its area greater than or less than the shape above? How do you know?

PART 5 How Long Are Names?

Mr. Moreno's class conducted two surveys in the fifth-grade class next door. The students collected two sets of data:

- The number of letters in their first names.
- The total number of letters in their first and last names.

As the class was just about finished graphing the data, the school bell rang. The next day they found that their data tables were mistakenly erased from the chalkboard. The graphs were still there. However, the students realized that they forgot to give each graph a title.

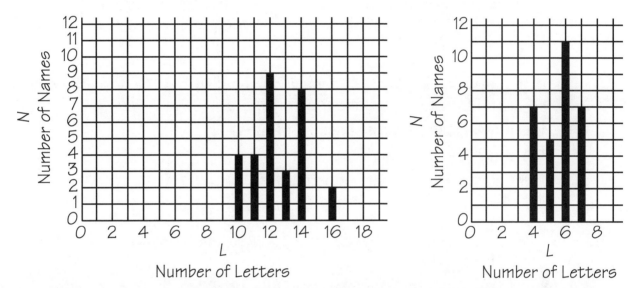

1. Write a title for each graph. Choose titles that will match each graph with the correct survey.

2. Describe each graph in words. Where are the bars? How tall are the bars?

3. Write a note to the class explaining how you were able to match the graphs with the two surveys.

4. Mr. Moreno's class collected data on the number of letters in their own first names. They made a graph titled, "Number of Letters in First Names in Two Classes." Describe this graph. Where are the bars? How tall are the bars?

PART 6 A Birthday Party

Solve the following problems. Choose an appropriate method for each: mental math, paper and pencil, or a calculator. Explain your solutions. Use a separate sheet of paper to show your work.

1. Today is Manny's birthday. He invited 19 of his friends to a pizza party at Cheesy Weesy Pizza. Each child will eat 3 slices of pizza. How many slices of pizza will they need? (Don't forget Manny.)

2. The menu reads as follows: Large Pizza (16 slices) $14.00; Medium Pizza (12 slices) $10.50; Small Pizza (8 slices) $8.00. List three possible orders that will feed the 20 children. Which of the three orders is the cheapest?

3. One-half of the children want cheese and sausage pizza. One-fourth want cheese pizza. One-fourth want pepperoni pizza.

   A. How many children want cheese and sausage?

   B. How many want cheese?

   C. How many children want pepperoni?

4. One-half of the children at the party drank two glasses of soda each. The rest drank 1 glass each.

   A. How many total glasses of soda did they drink?

   B. Manny's parents ordered pitchers of soda. If each pitcher of soda serves 5 glasses, how many pitchers were ordered?

   C. If one pitcher costs $1.75, what was the total cost for all of the pitchers of soda?

5. What was the total cost of the party? (Include the cheapest cost of the pizzas and the soda.)

6. Manny's grandfather gave Manny a $100 bill. Manny uses this money to pay for the party. He plans on putting the rest into his savings account. How much will Manny have left for his savings account?

Triangle Flash Card Master

- Make a flash card for each fact that is not circled on your *Multiplication* and *Division Facts I Know* charts. Write the product in the shaded corner of each triangle. Then cut out the flash cards.
- Your partner chooses one card at a time and covers one corner.
- To quiz you on a multiplication fact, your partner covers the shaded number. Multiply the two uncovered numbers.
- To quiz you on a division fact, your partner covers the number in the square or the number in the circle. Solve a division fact with the two uncovered numbers.
- Repeat the directions for your partner.

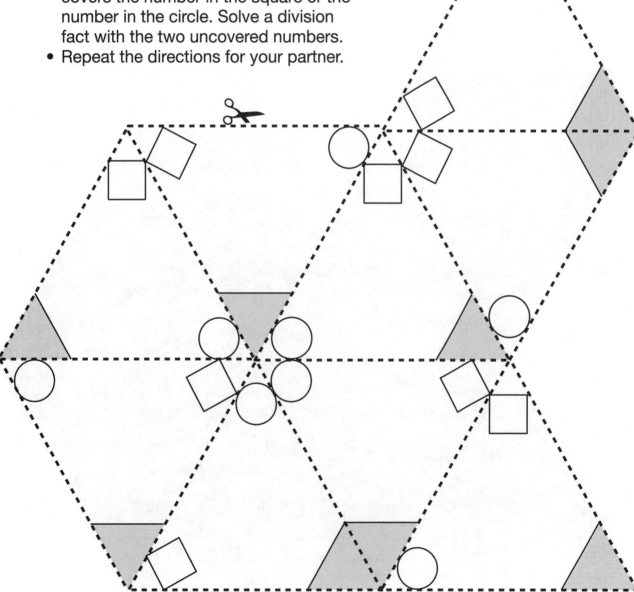

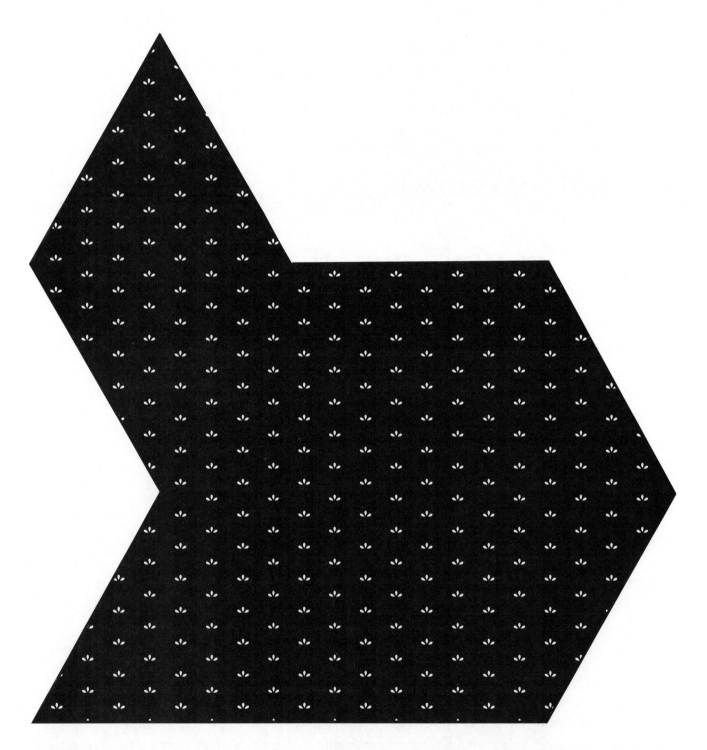

Triangle Flash Card Master

- Make a flash card for each fact that is not circled on your *Multiplication* and *Division Facts I Know* charts. Write the product in the shaded corner of each triangle. Then cut out the flash cards.
- Your partner chooses one card at a time and covers one corner.
- To quiz you on a multiplication fact, your partner covers the shaded number. Multiply the two uncovered numbers.
- To quiz you on a division fact, your partner covers the number in the square or the number in the circle. Solve a division fact with the two uncovered numbers.
- Repeat the directions for your partner.

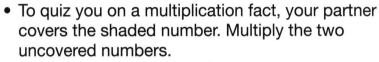

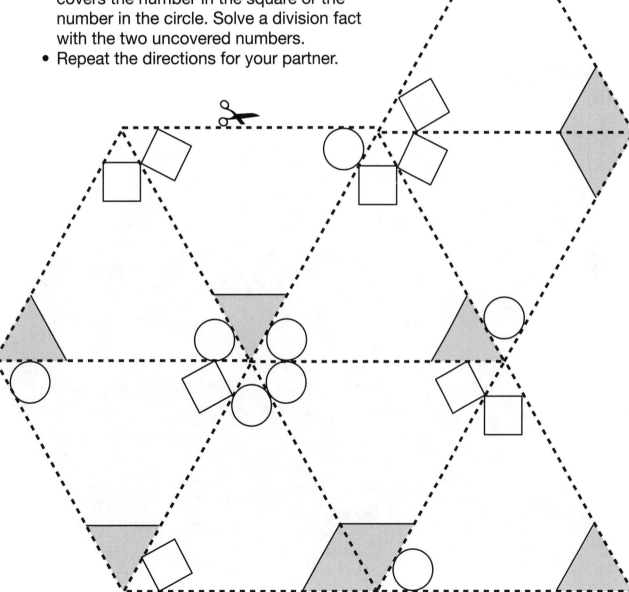

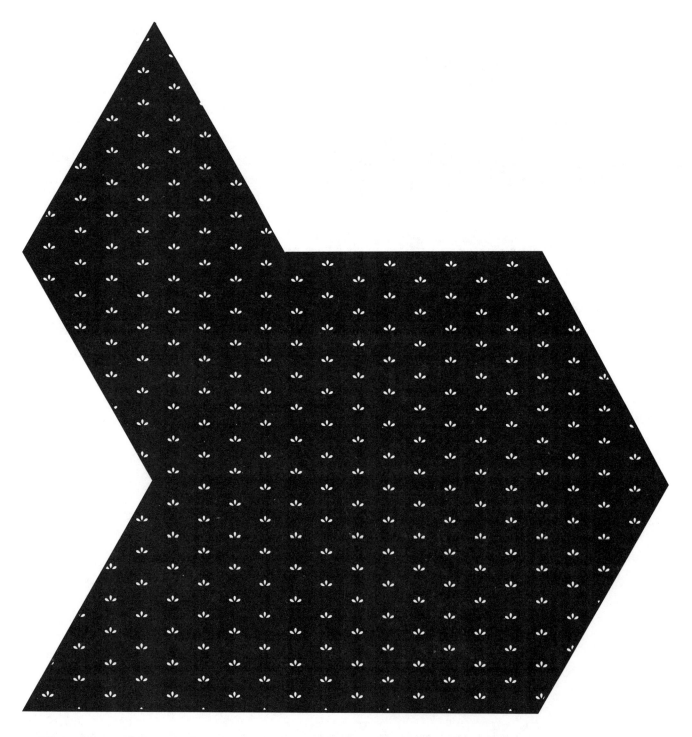

Experiment Review Chart

Experiment / Elements			
Main Variables			
Fixed Variables			
Variables Measured (units)			
Number of Trials			
Type of Graph			
Important Questions (Answers may vary.)			

Experiment / Elements			
Main Variables			
Fixed Variables			
Variables Measured (units)			
Number of Trials			
Type of Graph			
Important Questions (Answers may vary.)			

Three in a Row

Players

This is a game for two players.

Materials

- one calculator per player
- 8–10 game markers or tokens of one color or shape for each player
- one factor frame and product board per student pair

Rules

1. Player One selects two factors from the factor frame and finds their product with a calculator. He or she may select two different factors or use the same factor twice.
2. One of the player's markers is placed on the product board on the square with the number that is closest to the product of the two factors.
3. Player Two chooses two factors and follows the same steps described above.
4. Two markers may not occupy the same space.
5. The game continues until one player has three markers in a row, horizontally, vertically, or diagonally.

Game Board

Factor Frame

| 0.493 | 0.109 | 4.93 | 109 | 49.3 | 0.01 | 493 |

Product Board

10	500	2500	5
250	0.05	1	25,000
5000	50,000	25	50
$2\frac{1}{2}$	0.005	$\frac{1}{1000}$	$\frac{1}{2}$

Life Spans Data Tables

1858 Data Table

A Age (in years)	N Number of Deaths		Fraction of Deaths	Percent of Deaths (to the Nearest Percent)
	Tallies	Number		

1997 Data Table

A Age (in years)	N Number of Deaths		Fraction of Deaths	Percent of Deaths (to the Nearest Percent)
	Tallies	Number		

Soap Bubbles Data Table

Life Spans of Soap Bubbles

t Time in Seconds	Tallies	N Number of Bubbles	P Percent of Bubbles

Unit 9

Connections to Division

	Student Guide	Discovery Assignment Book	Adventure Book	Unit Resource Guide*
Lesson 1				
Fractions and Division	●	●		
Lesson 2				
Division	●	●		
Lesson 3				
Multiplication Methods	●	●		
Lesson 4				
Understanding Remainders	●			●
Lesson 5				
Calculator Strategies: Division	●			
Lesson 6				
Grass Act	●			●

Unit Resource Guide pages are from the teacher materials.

Unit 9 Home Practice

PART 1 Division Practice

Solve each problem using paper and pencil. Estimate to see if your answers are reasonable. Explain your estimation strategy for Question A.

A. $5762 \div 8 =$ **B.** $1263 \div 9 =$

C. $4691 \div 3 =$ **D.** $3189 \div 3 =$

PART 2 Fractions and Decimals

1. Find a pair of equivalent fractions in each set. You may use a calculator or another strategy. Be prepared to explain your thinking.

   A. $\frac{7}{15}$ $\frac{28}{75}$ $\frac{79}{160}$ $\frac{21}{45}$

   B. $\frac{15}{20}$ $\frac{125}{200}$ $\frac{3}{5}$ $\frac{27}{45}$

   C. $\frac{1}{3}$ $\frac{33}{100}$ $\frac{4}{5}$ $\frac{11}{33}$

   D. $\frac{6}{16}$ $\frac{24}{36}$ $\frac{36}{112}$ $\frac{66}{176}$

2. Use your calculator to change each fraction to a decimal (to the nearest hundredth). Then change each decimal to a percent.

	Decimal	Percent
A. $\frac{4}{5}$	_____	_____
B. $\frac{7}{12}$	_____	_____
C. $\frac{4}{15}$	_____	_____

PART 3 Multiplication and Division Practice

Solve the following problems using paper and pencil or mental math.
Estimate each answer to be sure it is reasonable.

A. $63 \times 45 =$

B. $221 \div 6 =$

C. $35 \times 29 =$

D. $8406 \div 23 =$

E. $0.52 \times 0.5 =$

F. $918 \div 54 =$

G. $0.83 \times 27 =$

H. $4500 \div 15 =$

I. $12{,}744 \div 68 =$

PART 4 Using Remainders

Solve each of the problems below. Show how you solved each one. Be sure to label the numbers you use, especially your answers.

Four hundred seventy-eight students from Bessie Coleman School are going to the Lizardland Amusement Park for a day.

1. At the Lizardland Amusement Park the roller coaster has 15 cars. Each car holds 4 people. What is the least number of times it will have to run to give all 478 students a ride?

2. Hot pretzels come in packages of 24. The pretzel stand will prepare two pretzels for each student. The workers at the stand will eat the rest of the pretzels. How many will the workers get to eat?

3. The park workers are putting up banners to welcome the school. They use a whole roll of paper that is 200 feet long for the banners. If they make 16 signs, how long will each sign be?

4. The Lizardland train has cars that can carry 18 passengers. If 250 people are riding the train, how many cars will be full?

5. For each of the problems, write any remainder as a mixed number.

   A. $425 \div 15 =$ **B.** $3500 \div 50 =$ **C.** $4005 \div 18 =$

PART 5 Solving Problems

Choose an appropriate method to solve each of the following problems. For each question, you may choose to use paper and pencil, mental math, or a calculator. Use a separate sheet of paper to explain how you solved each problem. (*Hint:* Drawing a picture may help you solve some of the problems.)

1. Penny's Pencil Company donated a case of pencils to Bessie Coleman Elementary School. The case contains 48 packs of pencils. Each pack contains 24 pencils. The principal wants to divide the pencils equally among 30 classrooms. How many pencils will each classroom receive? How many pencils will be left over for the office?

2. Mr. Moreno is putting together blank research journals for the fifth grade. Each journal needs 7 sheets of paper. Mr. Moreno has 2 packages of paper to use for the journals. How many journals can he make if one package of paper has 144 sheets?

3. The school is sponsoring a cultural fair. The fifth graders are arranging tables and chairs for a refreshment area at the fair. Half of the tables will seat 8 people. Half of the tables will seat 6 people. They have 112 chairs. How many of each kind of table will they set up?

4. One of the classes is serving burritos at the cultural fair. They will use 3 ounces of cheese on each burrito. How many burritos can they make if they have 5 pounds of cheese? (1 pound = 16 ounces)

5. During the cultural fair a group of students will demonstrate an Irish dance. There are 130 chairs available for the audience. The chairs are arranged into 8 equal rows. How many chairs are in each row? How many extra chairs will there be?

6. **A.** At the end of the fair, one group of students found that they served 384 egg rolls. The egg rolls came in boxes of 18. How many boxes of egg rolls did they need?

   B. The extra egg rolls were given to the volunteers. How many egg rolls did the volunteers get to share?

   C. If each volunteer got the same number of egg rolls and there were 12 volunteers, how many egg rolls did each volunteer get?

7. **A.** Mr. Moreno took 78 pictures at the cultural fair. He wanted to arrange the pictures in an album. Each page of his album holds 8 pictures. How many pages of his album can he completely fill?

   B. How many pages will he have to use in all?

Dividing Pizzas

1. Lin is planning a sleep-over. Her mother says she can invite 3 girls to spend the night so there will be 4 girls in all. Lin wants to order pizzas, but is not sure how many to order. Answer the following questions. Draw a picture when it helps.

   A. If Lin orders one pizza and the girls split it evenly, what fraction of the pizza will each of the girls get?

   B. Write the division number sentence that this fraction represents. Use the boxes as a guide.

$$\square \div \square = \frac{\square}{\square}$$

2. A. If Lin orders three pizzas and the girls split them fairly, what fraction of one pizza will each girl get?

   B. Write the division number sentence that this fraction represents. Use the boxes as a guide.

$$\square \div \square = \frac{\square}{\square}$$

3. The table below shows what happens when you share four pizzas with more and more people. Complete each column. Draw pictures when it helps.

Sharing Pizzas

Number of Pizzas	Number of People	Number of Pizzas Each Person Will Get	Division Number Sentence
4	1		
4	2		$4 \div 2 = 2$
4	3		
4	4	$\dfrac{4 \text{ pizzas}}{4 \text{ people}} =$ 1 pizza per person	
4	5		
4	10		
4	20		

4. Look at the chart. Describe the patterns you see.

Estimation and Division

Estimate each quotient. Tell what strategy you used to make your estimate.

Example: 22 | 834‾

Think:

22 × 10 =	220
22 × 20 =	440
22 × 30 =	660
22 × 40 =	880

←—834

Answer: I used multiples of 10. Since 834 is between 22 × 30 = 660 and 22 × 40 = 880, the quotient will be at least 30 but less than 40.

I. 11 | 258‾

2. 21 | 753‾

3. 32 | 568‾

4. 25 | 648‾

5. 42 | 3253‾

6. 38 | 6206‾

7. 50 | 792‾

8. 73 | 7890‾

More Estimation and Division

Estimate each quotient. Tell what strategy you used to make your estimate.

Example: 27 | 8432

Think:

25 × 200 =	5000
25 × 300 =	7500
25 × 400 =	10,000

←— 8432

Possible answer: Use 25 as a convenient number for 27. I tried multiples of 100. Since 8432 is between 25 × 300 and 25 × 400, the quotient is between 300 and 400.

1. 12 | 497

2. 79 | 9898

3. 52 | 6449

4. 26 | 8970

5. 17 | 874

6. 32 | 9583

Lattice Multiplication Practice

Use lattice multiplication to find the products. Estimate the product to see if your answer is reasonable.

1. Professor Peabody started to use lattice multiplication to find 6789×6. Finish the problem for him.

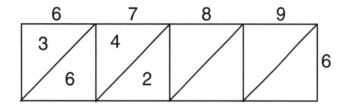

2. Finish Professor Peabody's new problem.

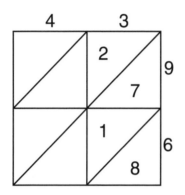

3. $35 \times 45 =$

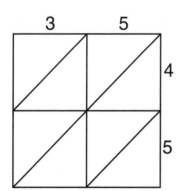

4. $764 \times 63 =$

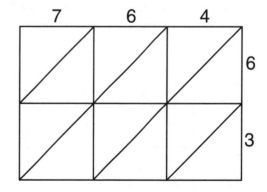

Draw your own lattices for Questions 5 and 6. Then solve the problems.

5. $28 \times 79 =$ **6.** $953 \times 57 =$

For Questions 7 and 8, make up two of your own multiplication problems and solve them using lattice multiplication. Check your answer using another method.

7. 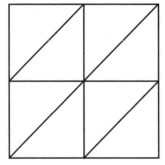   **8.**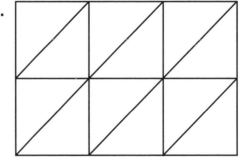

Unit 10

Maps and Coordinates

	Student Guide	Discovery Assignment Book	Adventure Book	Unit Resource Guide*
Lesson 1				
Negative Numbers	●			
Lesson 2				
Introducing Cartesian Coordinates	●			
Lesson 3				
Wherefore Art Thou, Romeo?			●	
Lesson 4				
Mr. Origin	●	●		●
Lesson 5				
Plotting Shapes	●			
Lesson 6				
These Boots Are Made for Sliding	●	●		
Lesson 7				
These Boots Are Made for Flipping	●	●		●
Lesson 8				
Reading a Map	●			●
Lesson 9				
Escher Drawings	●			

Unit Resource Guide pages are from the teacher materials.

Unit 10 Home Practice

PART 1 Division Practice

Solve the following problems using a paper-and-pencil method or mental math. Write your answers with remainders when necessary.

A. 589 ÷ 4 =   **B.** 6780 ÷ 5 =

C. 1239 ÷ 62 =   **D.** 42,000 ÷ 70 =

PART 2 Negative Numbers

1. Skip count by 2s backward from 10 to -10. Write the numbers on the number line as you count. Begin this way: 10, 8, 6, . . .

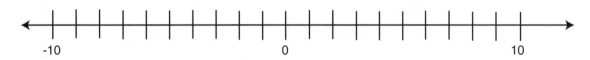

2. Skip count by 3s backward from 12 to -12. Write the numbers as you count.

3. Skip count forward from -20 to 20 by 4s. Write the numbers as you count. Begin this way: -20, -16, -12, ...

4. Use the number line below to show how you can find the answer to this problem: The temperature is -15°F. If the temperature rises 7 degrees, what will the temperature be?

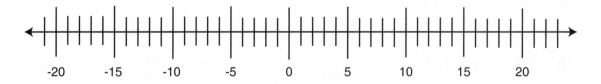

PART 3 Working with Coordinates

1. Name the coordinates of point T on the graph. _____

2. Plot three other points on the graph so that you can form a rectangle when you connect the points. Label each with a letter.

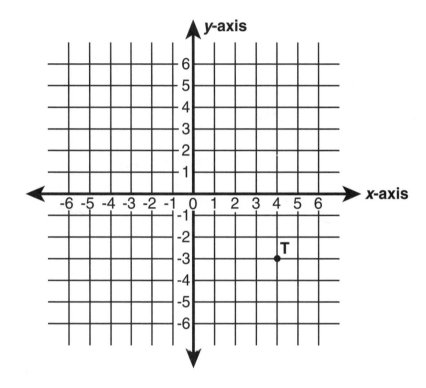

3. Use ordered pairs to list the coordinates of the three points you plotted.

PART 4 Order of Operations

Solve the problems following the order of operations.

1. $30 \times 30 - 300 =$ 2. $1000 - 20 \times 20 =$

3. $(70 + 20) \times 200 =$ 4. $2000 \div 40 + 60 =$

5. $125 - 120 \div 20 =$ 6. $3900 - 8 \times 200 =$

7. $1400 \div 200 + 238 =$ 8. $900 + 700 \div 100 =$

PART 5 Practicing the Operations

Solve the following problems using a paper-and-pencil method. Estimate to be sure your answer is reasonable.

I. **A.** $2.3 \times 68 =$

   B. $261 \times 90 =$

   C. $85 \times 98 =$

   D. $\$7.87 + \$26.67 =$

   E. $2098 \div 12 =$

   F. $547 - 168 =$

   G. $0.04 \times 7.2 =$

   H. $3399 \div 43 =$

   I. $8730 - 483 =$

2. Explain your estimation strategies for Questions 1A and 1B.

PART 6 Sunny Vacation

Choose an appropriate method to solve each of the following problems. For some questions you may need to find an exact answer, while for others you may only need an estimate. For each question, you may choose to use paper and pencil, mental math, or a calculator. Use a separate sheet of paper to explain how you solved each problem.

1. Brett and Reggie plan to fly away to Faraway Island. The Get-Up-And-Go Travel Agency has a sale in progress. If you buy one round trip ticket for $899.99, you will get a second ticket free. Global Travel is offering round trip tickets to Faraway Island for $452.99. Which travel agency offers the best deal for Brett and Reggie? Why?

2. Joanne is going to Faraway Island by herself for seven days. She has $2000 to spend. If she buys one airline ticket from Global Travel, about how much money can she spend each day?

3. Nicole won a free airline ticket to Faraway Island. She has $1000 to spend while she is there.

   A. Nicole plans to spend $\frac{1}{2}$ of the money on hotel accommodations. It costs $79 per night to stay at the Sunset Beach Lodge. Is it within Nicole's budget to stay at the lodge for 6 nights?

   B. If Nicole plans to spend $\frac{1}{2}$ of the money on hotel accommodations and $\frac{1}{4}$ of it on food, about how much money will she have left to spend on souvenirs and entertainment?

4. Lucky Louise went bargain hunting. She found a fan for $0.65, 7 matching pens for $0.15 apiece, and a special on pencils—5 for $1.60. If she buys 2 fans, all 7 matching pens, and only 3 pencils, how much money will she spend?

5. As Brett and Reggie board the plane to return home, the temperature on Faraway Island is 90°F. Brett must return to Minneapolis where it is -10°F. Reggie must return to Milwaukee where it is -7°F.

   A. Where is it colder, Minneapolis or Milwaukee? How much colder?

   B. What is the difference in temperature between Minneapolis and Faraway Island?

Label the Axes

Look at the direction Mr. Origin is facing in the pictures below. For each drawing, label both the *x*- and *y*-axis. In addition, fill in the ovals to show the positive and negative directions.

I.

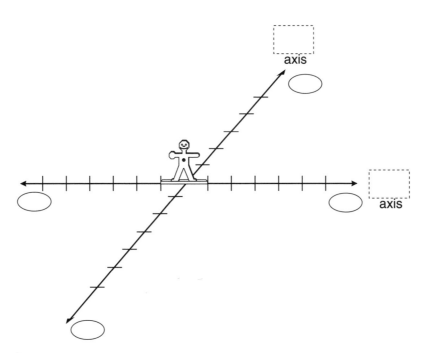

2.

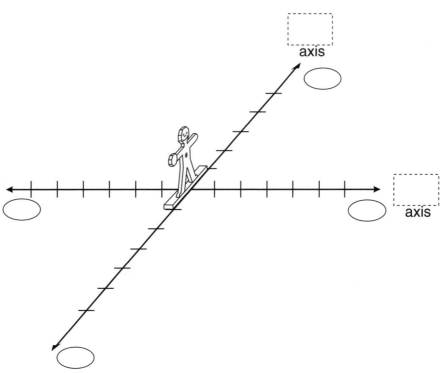

Slides

José, the Master Shape Maker, decided to experiment with ordered pairs of coordinates. This is the order for a shape that he received:

Order:
(1, 3)   (2, 6)   (2, 2)

José drew the shape like so:

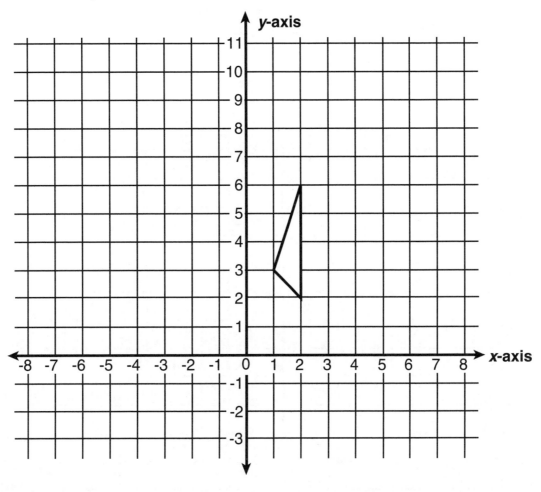

José wondered what the shape would look like if he added 5 to each of the x-coordinates.

1. Add 5 to each x-coordinate and record your new coordinates in the table. Then draw the new shape on the grid above. Label the points on the new triangle and the old triangle with their coordinates.

Old Shape	New Shape
(1, 3)	
(2, 6)	
(2, 2)	

2. Describe what happened to the triangle:

José wondered what would happen if he added 5 to each *y*-coordinate of the original triangle.

3. Add 5 to each *y*-coordinate. Record the new coordinates in the table. Then draw the new shape and label the points of the new triangle and the old triangle with their coordinates.

Old Shape	New Shape
(1, 3)	
(2, 6)	
(2, 2)	

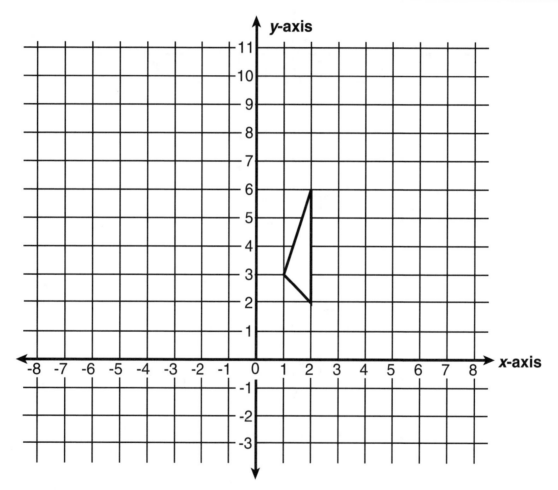

4. Describe what happened to the triangle:

José drew the gray boot. The heel is at (2, 1). The toe is at (4, 2) and the top front is at (3, 5). He then slid the boot over. The white boot shows where the boot is after the slide.

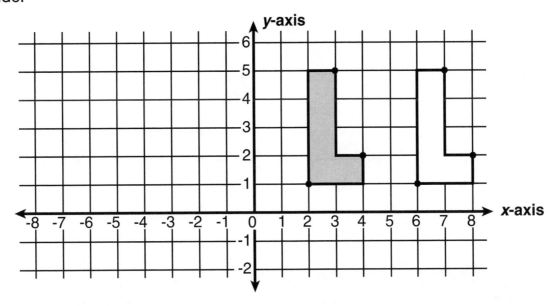

5. How did the boot move?

6. Fill in the missing coordinates:

Boot	Heel Coordinates	Toe Coordinates	Top Front Coordinates
Gray Boot	(2, 1)	(4, 2)	(3, 5)
White Boot			

7. Which coordinate changed? (*x* or *y*)

8. Which coordinate did not change? (*x* or *y*)

Name _____ **Date** _____

Use these figures to explore slides in Questions 9–11. Record the coordinates in the charts.

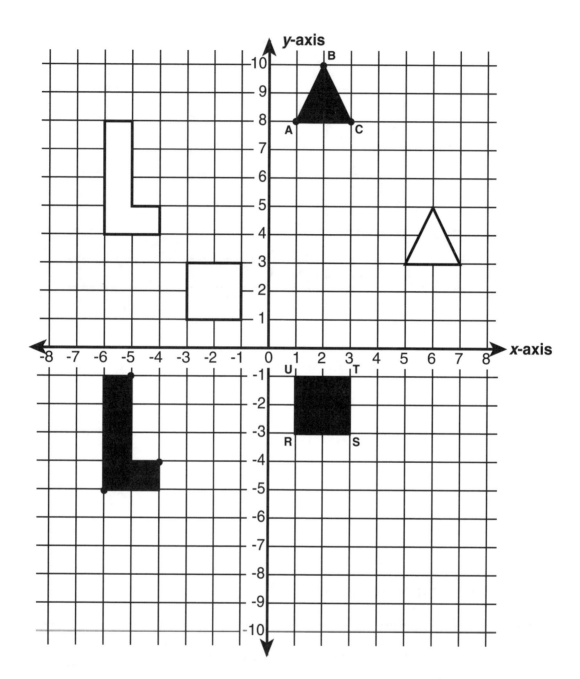

These Boots Are Made for Sliding

9. The black boot shows the starting position.

Boot	Heel Coordinates	Toe Coordinates	Top Front Coordinates
Black Boot			
White Boot			

Explain how the coordinates changed.

10. The black triangle shows the starting position.

Triangle	Vertex A Coordinates	Vertex B Coordinates	Vertex C Coordinates
Black Triangle			
White Triangle			

Explain how the coordinates changed.

11. The black square shows the starting position.

Square	Vertex R Coordinates	Vertex S Coordinates	Vertex T Coordinates	Vertex U Coordinates
Black Square				
White Square				

Explain how the coordinates changed.

Flips

1. Flip the shapes over the *y*-axis and draw the image. Label the corresponding vertices with the appropriate letters. To check your work, you can fold your paper along the *y*-axis. The two shapes should match exactly.

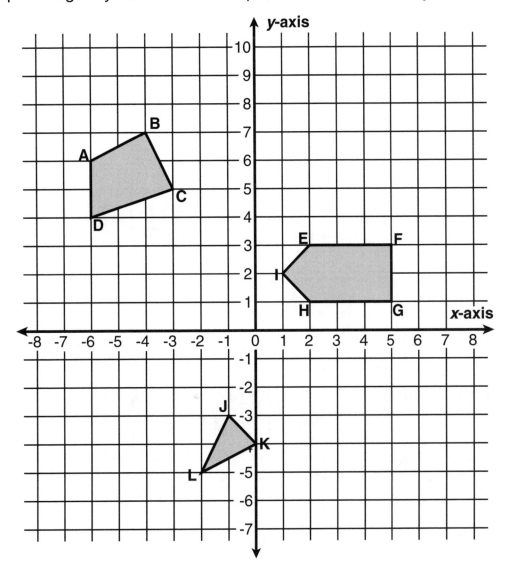

Name _____   Date _____

2. Flip these shapes over the *x*-axis and draw the image of each shape. Label the corresponding vertices with the appropriate letters. To check your work, you can fold your paper along the *x*-axis.

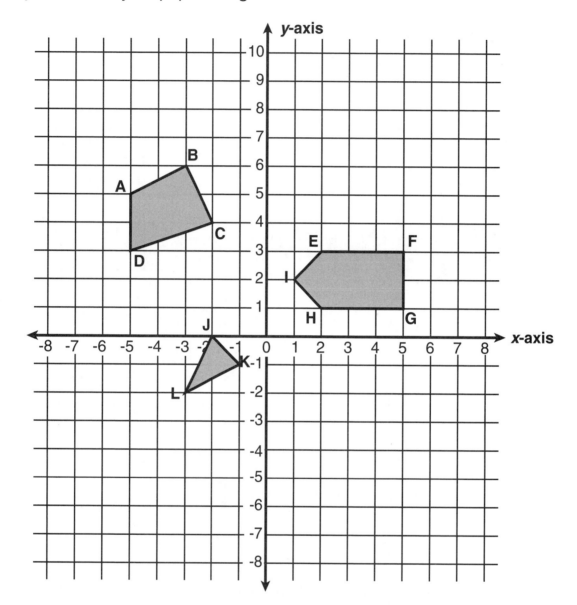

These Boots Are Made for Flipping

Unit 11

Number Patterns, Primes, and Fractions

	Student Guide	Discovery Assignment Book	Adventure Book	Unit Resource Guide*
Lesson 1				
Factor 40	●	●		
Lesson 2				
Sifting for Primes	●	●		
Lesson 3				
Patterns with Square Numbers	●			
Lesson 4				
Finding Prime Factors	●	●		
Lesson 5				
Comparing Fractions	●			
Lesson 6				
Reducing Fractions	●			●
Lesson 7				
A Further Look at Patterns and Primes				●
Lesson 8				
From Factors to Fractions	●			

Unit Resource Guide pages are from the teacher materials.

175

Unit 11 Home Practice

PART 1 Multiplication and Division Practice

Use paper and pencil to solve the following problems. Estimate to be sure your answers are reasonable.

1. **A.** $2170 \div 52 =$ **B.** $28 \times 69 =$

   C. $1307 \times 9 =$ **D.** $9603 \div 3 =$

2. Explain your estimation strategies for Questions 1A and 1C.

PART 2 Going to the Theater

Arti and Lin helped collect tickets at Arti's mother's theater. Tickets for the play are $14 for adults and $9 for students. Adult theater members get a discount and only have to pay half-price ($7).

Number of Tickets in Each Category

Performance	Adult Tickets (full price)	Student Tickets	Adult Member Tickets
Friday	97	15	13
Saturday	103	21	20
Sunday	82	43	5

1. How many people attended each performance of the play?

2. Find the amount of money collected for each performance.

3. How many more adults than students saw the play?

PART 3 Using Exponents

1. Each of the three numbers below is written as a product of primes. Rewrite the prime factorizations using exponents.

   A. $180 = 2 \times 3 \times 5 \times 2 \times 3 =$ _____

   B. $2125 = 5 \times 17 \times 5 \times 5 =$ _____

   C. $17{,}820 = 11 \times 2 \times 3 \times 3 \times 5 \times 2 \times 3 \times 3 =$ _____

2. Write each of the following numbers as a product of its primes without exponents. Use factor trees. Then write the number as a product of its primes using exponents.

   A. 20   **B.** 48   **C.** 56

PART 4 Fractions

1. Reduce the following fractions to lowest terms.

   A. $\dfrac{14}{28}$ **B.** $\dfrac{24}{42}$ **C.** $\dfrac{60}{200}$ **D.** $\dfrac{27}{90}$ **E.** $\dfrac{57}{120}$

2. Solve the following. First, find common denominators and then add or subtract. Reduce your answers to lowest terms.

   A. $\dfrac{4}{5} - \dfrac{3}{10} =$ **B.** $\dfrac{2}{5} - \dfrac{1}{15} =$ **C.** $\dfrac{5}{6} + \dfrac{1}{24} =$

NUMBER PATTERNS, PRIMES, AND FRACTIONS

PART 5 Practicing Computation

1. Solve the following problems using paper and pencil. Estimate to be sure your answers are reasonable. Explain your estimation strategies.

   A. $46 \times 23 =$ **B.** $372 \times 9 =$

2. Solve the following problems using a paper-and-pencil method. Express quotients as mixed numbers.

   A. $3850 \times 5 =$ **B.** $2076 \div 9 =$ **C.** $78 \times 19 =$

   D. $5945 + 6148 =$ **E.** $9035 - 2747 =$ **F.** $2703 \div 13 =$

PART 6 The Band

Choose an appropriate method to solve each of the following problems. For some questions you may need to find an exact answer, while for others you may only need an estimate. For each question, you may choose to use paper and pencil, mental math, or a calculator. Use a separate sheet of paper to explain how you solved each problem.

1. The Krinkles, a pop rock band from Chicago, recently toured the United States. Their tour van can travel about 12 miles on 1 gallon of gas. They bought about 200 gallons of gas on their tour. About how many miles did they travel?

2. If gas costs $1.50 per gallon, how much did the Krinkles spend on gas during their tour?

3. The Krinkles tour lasted 20 days. Each day the Krinkles budgeted $20 per person for food and $45 per person for a motel room. There are 5 members in the band. What was the total amount of money the band budgeted to spend on food, motel rooms, and gas?

4. On average, 300 people came to each of their concerts. Tickets were $5.00 per person at every concert.

   A. If they performed each of the 20 days of the tour, about how many people saw the Krinkles on tour?

   B. About how much money did they collect?

   C. After paying for gas, motels, and food, about how much money was left to pay the band?

   D. About how much did each member make?

   E. About how much did each band member make each day?

Factor 40 Game Board

Factor 40

1	2	3	4	5	6	7	8
9	10	11	12	13	14	15	16
17	18	19	20	21	22	23	24
25	26	27	28	29	30	31	32
33	34	35	36	37	38	39	40

Factor 40

1	2	3	4	5	6	7	8
9	10	11	12	13	14	15	16
17	18	19	20	21	22	23	24
25	26	27	28	29	30	31	32
33	34	35	36	37	38	39	40

200 Chart

1	2	3	4	5	6	7	8	9	10
11	12	13	14	15	16	17	18	19	20
21	22	23	24	25	26	27	28	29	30
31	32	33	34	35	36	37	38	39	40
41	42	43	44	45	46	47	48	49	50
51	52	53	54	55	56	57	58	59	60
61	62	63	64	65	66	67	68	69	70
71	72	73	74	75	76	77	78	79	80
81	82	83	84	85	86	87	88	89	90
91	92	93	94	95	96	97	98	99	100
101	102	103	104	105	106	107	108	109	110
111	112	113	114	115	116	117	118	119	120
121	122	123	124	125	126	127	128	129	130
131	132	133	134	135	136	137	138	139	140
141	142	143	144	145	146	147	148	149	150
151	152	153	154	155	156	157	158	159	160
161	162	163	164	165	166	167	168	169	170
171	172	173	174	175	176	177	178	179	180
181	182	183	184	185	186	187	188	189	190
191	192	193	194	195	196	197	198	199	200

Factor Trees

1. **A.** Complete each of these factor trees for 24.

B. Factor 24 into primes.

C. Write 24 as a product of its prime factors using exponents.

2. **A.** Make two different factor trees for 36.

B. Factor 36 into primes.

C. Write 36 as a product of its prime factors using exponents.

Unit 12

Using Fractions

	Student Guide	Discovery Assignment Book	Adventure Book	Unit Resource Guide*
Lesson 1				
Hexagon Duets	●	●		
Lesson 2				
Adding Mixed Numbers	●			
Lesson 3				
Fractions of Groups	●			
Lesson 4				
Multiplication of Fractions	●	●		
Lesson 5				
Using Patterns to Multiply Fractions	●			
Lesson 6				
Peanut Soup			●	
Lesson 7				
Party Problems	●			
Lesson 8				
Midterm Test				●

Unit Resource Guide pages are from the teacher materials.

187

Unit 12 Home Practice

PART 1 Multiplication and Division Practice

Use a paper-and-pencil method to solve the following problems. Write any remainders as fractions in lowest terms.

I. A. $8967 \div 6 =$ B. $5875 \div 50 =$

    C. $246 \times 9 =$ D. $2400 \div 30 =$

    E. $105 \times 4 =$

2. Can you solve any of the above problems using mental math? If so, explain your strategies.

PART 2 Division Practice

I. Solve the following problems in your head or with paper and pencil. Write the quotient as a mixed number. Reduce all fractions to lowest terms.

    A. $33 \div 4 =$ B. $76 \div 9 =$ C. $17 \div 2 =$

    D. $108 \div 10 =$ E. $54 \div 7 =$ F. $41 \div 6 =$

    G. $42 \div 8 =$ H. $23 \div 6 =$ I. $67 \div 8 =$

2. Use a calculator to find the answers to the following. Write your answers as mixed numbers. Reduce all fractions to lowest terms.

    A. $1388 \div 16 =$ B. $18,478 \div 24 =$ C. $43,956 \div 32 =$

PART 3 Fractions

Solve the following problems. Estimate to see if your answers are reasonable.

1. A. $\frac{1}{3} \times 15 =$ B. $\frac{1}{8} \times 24 =$ C. $\frac{2}{3} \times \frac{1}{6} =$

    D. $\frac{1}{5} \times \frac{5}{6} =$ E. $\frac{1}{12} \times \frac{2}{5} =$ F. $\frac{3}{8} \times 16 =$

    G. $\frac{1}{4}$ of $2.00 =$ H. $\frac{2}{5}$ of $50 =$ I. $\frac{3}{4}$ of $24 =$

2. Solve Question 1D a different way. Explain your strategy.

PART 4 Analyze the Class

In a class of 24 students:

1. Of the students, 25% are left-handed. How many students are left-handed?

2. One-third of the class is wearing jeans. How many students are wearing jeans?

3. Extra credit math work was done by 18 students. What fraction of the class did extra credit work?

4. What percent of the class did extra credit work?

5. Twelve students are girls. What fraction of students are boys?

PART 5 Let's Practice

Use paper and pencil to solve the following. Use a separate sheet of paper to show your work.

A. $3\frac{4}{5} + 7\frac{1}{4} =$ **B.** $862 \times 9 =$ **C.** $94 \times 34 =$

D. $53.68 + 0.432 =$ **E.** $7341 \div 9 =$ **F.** $82 - 14.65 =$

PART 6 Working with Coordinates

1. A. Plot the coordinates in the table. Record the ordered pairs. Label the points with a letter on the graph.

Point	x-coordinate	y-coordinate	Ordered Pairs
A	-2	-1	
B	-3	-3	
C	-1	-3	
D	1	3	

B. You will need a ruler for this problem.

If 1 cm = 200 cm on the graph, what is the distance between A and D?

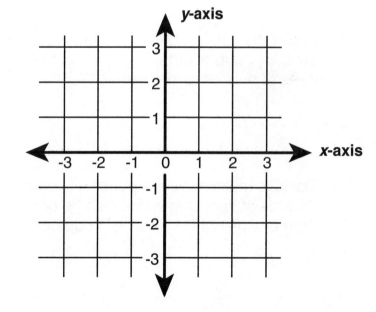

PART 7 Food for Thought

Solve the following problems. You may use any of the tools you have used in class such as calculators, drawings, or pattern blocks. Show your solutions.

1. **A.** If three friends split $1\frac{1}{2}$ pizzas evenly, how much of a whole pizza will each person eat?

   B. If six friends split $1\frac{1}{2}$ pizzas, how much of a whole pizza will each person eat?

2. Michael's father made a pumpkin pie. Michael and his brother couldn't wait until after dinner to eat the pie. Michael ate $\frac{1}{8}$ of the pie. His brother ate $\frac{1}{4}$ of the pie. What fraction of the whole pie was left for dessert after dinner?

3. Ana is making nut bread for a bake sale. The recipe for one loaf of bread calls for $\frac{3}{4}$ cup of nuts. If she wants to make 5 loaves of bread, how many cups of nuts does she need?

4. David is making orange punch. He combines $5\frac{1}{4}$ cups of orange juice with $2\frac{2}{3}$ cups of sparkling water. Can he pour all the punch into a 2-quart pitcher? Why or why not? (1 quart = 4 cups)

5. A muffin recipe calls for $\frac{1}{3}$ cup of blueberries for each pan of muffins. If Blanca picked 3 cups of berries, how many pans of muffins can Blanca make?

Hexagon Duets Spinner

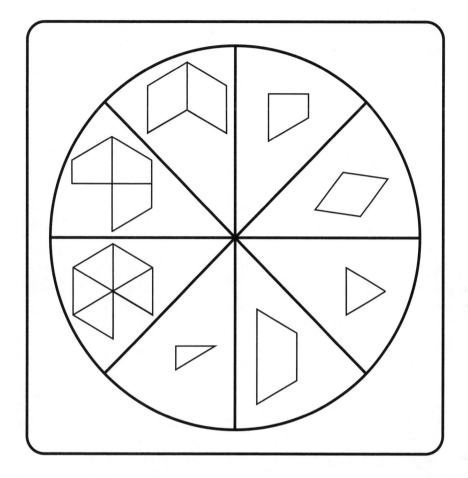

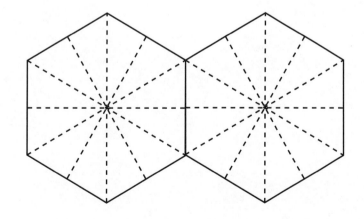

Pattern Block Record Sheet

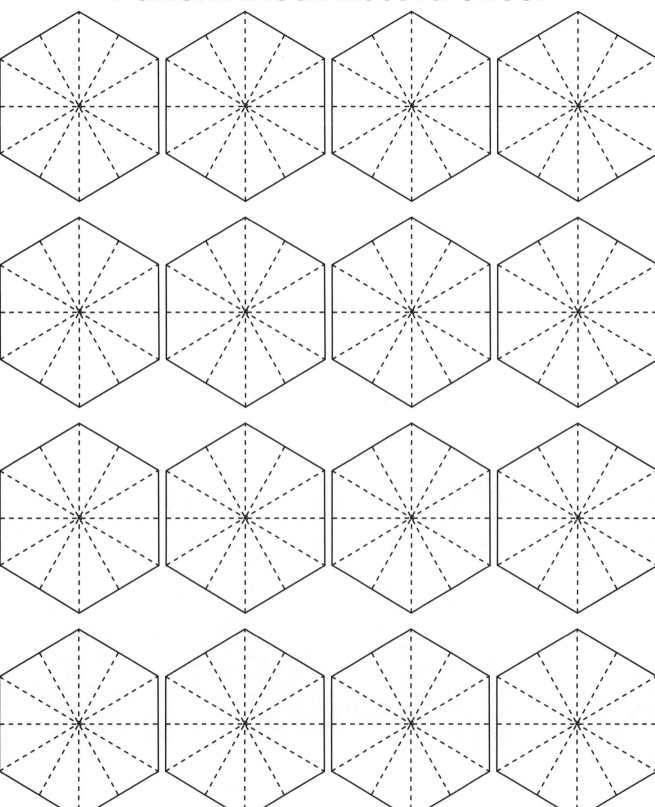

Pattern Block Record Sheet

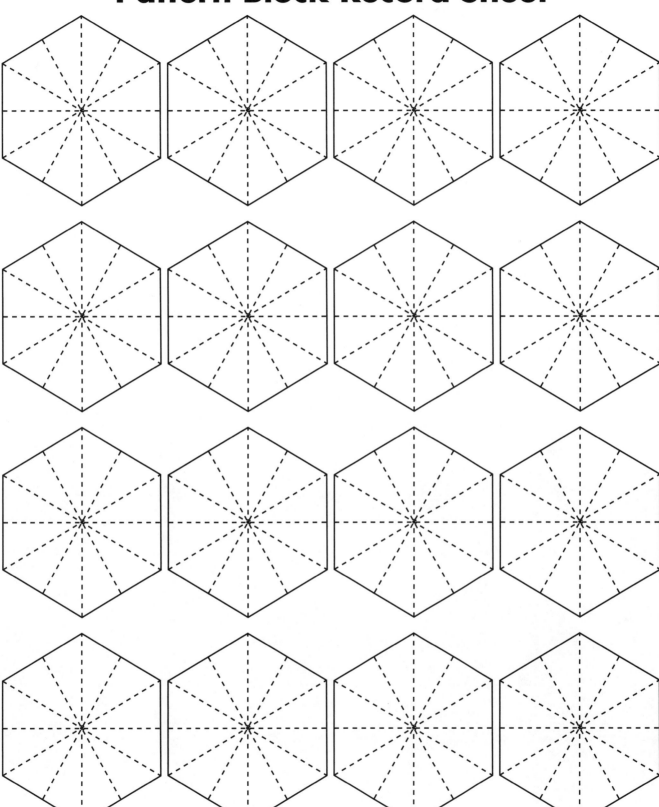

Unit 13

Ratio and Proportion

	Student Guide	Discovery Assignment Book	Adventure Book	Unit Resource Guide*
Lesson 1				
Ratios, Recipes, and Proportions	●			
Lesson 2				
Variables in Proportion	●			
Lesson 3				
Sink and Float	●	●		●
Lesson 4				
Mass vs. Volume: Proportions and Density	●			
Lesson 5				
Problems of Scale	●			●

Unit Resource Guide pages are from the teacher materials.

Feathers   Lead

Name _____   Date _____

Unit 13 Home Practice

PART 1 Division Practice

A. $45 \div 9 =$ **B.** $4 \div 2 =$ **C.** $10 \div 5 =$

D. $9 \div 3 =$ **E.** $60 \div 6 =$ **F.** $25 \div 5 =$

G. $40 \div 5 =$ **H.** $36 \div 6 =$ **I.** $30 \div 10 =$

J. $8 \div 4 =$ **K.** $20 \div 4 =$ **L.** $12 \div 6 =$

M. $80 \div 8 =$ **N.** $14 \div 2 =$ **O.** $90 \div 10 =$

PART 2 Fractions, Decimals, and Percents

I. Find n to make each pair of fractions equivalent.

A. $\dfrac{4}{5} = \dfrac{n}{20}$ **B.** $\dfrac{9}{10} = \dfrac{36}{n}$ **C.** $\dfrac{4}{n} = \dfrac{28}{49}$

D. $\dfrac{n}{8} = \dfrac{4}{32}$ **E.** $\dfrac{5}{6} = \dfrac{n}{36}$ **F.** $\dfrac{3}{4} = \dfrac{60}{n}$

RATIO AND PROPORTION

2. For each pair of numbers write a number sentence using <, >, and =. (*Hint:* Use a calculator to change the fractions to decimals.)

   A. $\frac{1}{6}$ and 30%   **B.** 65% and $\frac{5}{8}$ **C.** $\frac{4}{9}$ and 46%

   D. 0.66 and $\frac{2}{3}$ **E.** 0.43 and $\frac{3}{7}$ **F.** $\frac{6}{15}$ and 40%

PART 3 Computation Practice

Solve the following problems using paper and pencil. Estimate to be sure your answers are reasonable. Give your answers to division problems as mixed numbers. Use a separate sheet of paper if you need more space.

A. $87 \times 62 =$ **B.** $2.3 \times 52 =$ **C.** $1892 \div 5 =$

D. $3406 \div 27 =$ **E.** $4\frac{5}{6} + 3\frac{1}{5} =$ **F.** $\frac{11}{12} + 1\frac{2}{3} =$

G. $\frac{2}{3} \times 36 =$ **H.** $\frac{3}{5} \times \frac{5}{6} =$ **I.** $314.56 + .89 =$

J. $1089.23 - 17.9 =$ **K.** $58 - .36 =$ **L.** $173.4 + 38.65 =$

Name _____   Date _____

PART 4 Measuring the Density of Rocks
You will need a piece of graph paper to complete these questions.

1. On a geology field trip, Blanca found three rocks made of the same type of material. She measured the mass and volume of each rock. Her data table is shown at the right. Plot the data on a piece of graph paper. Put Mass (*M*) on the vertical axis and Volume (*V*) on the horizontal axis. Scale your axes so that *M* goes up to 100 g and *V* goes up to 30 cc.

Rock	Volume (cc)	Mass (g)
A	3	8.5
B	5	15
C	21	60

2. Use a point on the line to find the density for this kind of rock. Express the density as a ratio of mass to volume.

3. Remember, the density of water is $\frac{1g}{1\,cc}$ (or 1 g/cc). Compare the density of Blanca's rocks with the density of water. Would you expect the rocks to sink or float? Why?

4. On the field trip, Blanca also found a bigger rock of the same material. This rock is too big to fit in the graduated cylinder. She knows the mass of the rock is 80 grams. Use your graph to find the volume of this rock.

5. A rock made of the same material has a volume of 15 cc. What is its mass? Explain how you found your answer.

6. If a rock made of the same material has a volume of 40 cc, what is its mass? Show your solution strategy.

PART 5 In Proportion

Solve the following problems using pencil and paper or a calculator.

1. David and Felicia both brought chocolate chip cookies for dessert with their lunches.

   A. David counts 14 chips in his two cookies. What is the ratio of chips to cookies in David's lunch?

   B. Felicia counts 35 chips in her 5 cookies. What is the ratio of chips to cookies in Felicia's lunch?

   C. Who has the higher ratio of chocolate chips to cookies? Explain.

2. Notebooks are on sale for 3 for $1.29. Alexis's mother decides to stock up on them.

   A. If she buys nine notebooks, how much will she spend on notebooks?

   B. If she buys ten notebooks, how much will she spend? What does one notebook cost?

3. Candy bars come in packages of 5 for $2.00.
   A. What is the price for 15 candy bars?

   B. Give two different strategies you can use to solve the problem.

4. Arti is mixing some orange paint for the class mural. She mixes 3 squirts of yellow to 2 squirts of red and gets a beautiful orange color. Shannon put 9 squirts of yellow in her bowl. If she wants to get the same orange color as Arti, how many squirts of red should she use?

Sink and Float Tables

Sink and Float Data Table

Object	V Volume in cc	M Mass in g	Sink or Float?
water			——

Density of water as a ratio: _____

Density of water as a decimal: _____

Sinks in Water

Object	Density as Ratio $\frac{M}{V}$	Density as Decimal

Floats in Water

Object	Density as Ratio $\frac{M}{V}$	Density as Decimal

Unit 14

Using Circles

	Student Guide	Discovery Assignment Book	Adventure Book	Unit Resource Guide*
Lesson 1				
Exploring Circumference and Diameter	●	●		
Lesson 2				
Circumference vs. Diameter	●			●
Lesson 3				
Constructing Circles with Terry	●	●		
Lesson 4				
Complex Constructions	●			●
Lesson 5				
Circle Graphs	●	●		
Lesson 6				
Practice and Problems	●			

Unit Resource Guide pages are from the teacher materials.

Unit 14 Home Practice

PART 1 Division Practice

Use paper and pencil or mental math to solve the following problems. Estimate to be sure your answers are reasonable. Explain your estimation strategy for A.

A. $8965 \div 57 =$

B. $7682 \div 40 =$

C. $4128 \div 4 \div 2 =$

D. $4128 \div 8 =$

E. $7900 \div 10 =$

PART 2 Order of Operations

Solve the following problems following the order of operations. Use paper and pencil or mental math.

A. $18 \div 3 \times 7 =$

B. $15 + 24 + 4 =$

C. $350 - 210 \div 7 =$

D. $60 + 80 \times 7 =$

E. $7^2 \times 2^2 =$

F. $30 \times 80 \div 6 =$

G. $60 \times 80 + 1200 =$

H. $4500 \div 9 - 5 =$

I. $(130 + 150) \div 4 =$

Name _____ Date _____

PART 3 Circumference vs. Diameter

Professor Peabody estimated the circumference and the diameter of some circles. He recorded his estimates below. Some of his estimates are reasonable and some of them are crazy.

If the estimate is reasonable, circle "close enough." If the estimate is not reasonable, circle "crazy."

1. Diameter = 2 cm	Circumference = 6 cm	Close enough	Crazy
2. D = 36 cm	C = 12 cm	Close enough	Crazy
3. D = 15 cm	C = 30 cm	Close enough	Crazy
4. D = 24 cm	C = 75 cm	Close enough	Crazy
5. D = 30 cm	C = 900 cm	Close enough	Crazy
6. D = 123 cm	C = 1234 cm	Close enough	Crazy
7. D = 3211 cm	C = 9633 cm	Close enough	Crazy

PART 4 Function Machines

Here are two function machines. The first one takes the input number, adds 2 to it, and then multiplies the sum by 3. The second one takes the input number, multiplies it by 3, and then adds 2.

Complete both of the function machines.

Input N	Output $(N + 2) \times 3$
1	9
2	
	21
6	
9	
	30
12	
13	

Input N	Output $N \times 3 + 2$
1	5
2	
	14
7	
10	
	38
15	
20	

PART 5 Practicing the Operations

Use paper and pencil or mental math to solve the following. Write your answers to the division problems as mixed numbers.

A. $57 \times 3.9 =$

B. $4312 \div 6 =$

C. $\frac{3}{4} + \frac{5}{6} =$

D. $39 \times 4 =$

E. $\frac{11}{12} - \frac{3}{8} =$

F. $68 \times \frac{1}{4} =$

G. $376.2 + 78.36 =$

H. $1205.4 - 83.27 =$

I. $1835 \div 46 =$

J. $\frac{1}{8} \times \frac{2}{3} =$

K. $\frac{1}{2} \times \frac{8}{15} =$

L. $3\frac{4}{5} + 1\frac{1}{3} =$

PART 6 Planet Power

Choose an appropriate method to solve each of the following problems. For some questions you may need to find an exact answer, while for others you may only need an estimate. For each question, you may choose to use paper and pencil, mental math, or a calculator. Use a separate sheet of paper to explain how you solved each problem.

I. Today is the premiere of the new movie *Planet Power.* Twenty-seven fifth graders were invited to see the movie. Each student received a complimentary bag of popcorn. All the bags were the same size, but some contained more popcorn than others. Brandon's bag was $\frac{3}{4}$ full. Lee Yah's bag was $\frac{1}{2}$ full. John's bag was $\frac{5}{8}$ full, and Ana's bag was $\frac{1}{4}$ full.

A. Who had the most popcorn?

B. Who had the least?

2. Harvey makes the popcorn for the movie theater. He bought 2 boxes of butter for the popcorn. Each box contains 4 sticks of butter. If Harvey needs to use $1\frac{3}{4}$ boxes of butter, how many sticks will he use?

3. In the movie, two space explorers are shipwrecked on a desolate planet. They decide to split up and explore the planet. Their spacecraft contains 6 canteens. Three of the canteens are full of water and three canteens are $\frac{1}{2}$ full of water. If they divide the water supply equally, how much water will each explorer get?

4. After the movie the students were invited to a party to meet one of the cast members. At the party, the students were offered cake. Of the 27 children at the party, $\frac{2}{3}$ wanted a slice of yellow cake. The rest of the students wanted a slice of chocolate cake.

A. How many children wanted yellow cake?

B. How many children wanted chocolate cake?

C. If each cake is cut into 6 equal pieces, how many chocolate cakes are needed?

D. How many yellow cakes are needed?

Gluing It Down

You will need glue, scissors, and string to complete this page. Cut several pieces of string that are the same length as the diameter of the circle below. Glue or tape the pieces of string around the circumference of the circle.

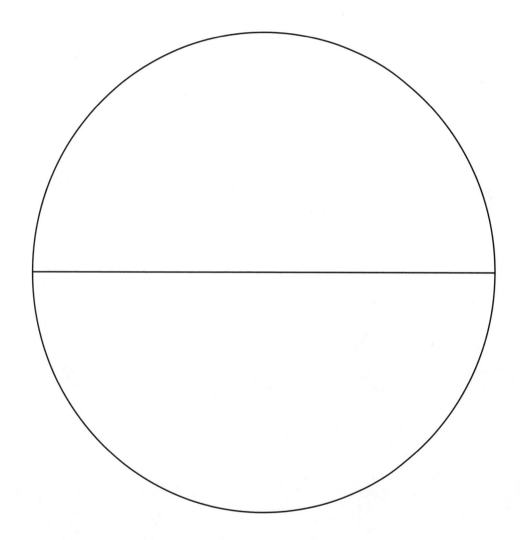

1. How many diameters are needed to fit around the circumference?

2. Lin did this activity with a smaller circle. She cut several pieces of string the length of the diameter of a smaller circle and glued them around the circumference of the smaller circle. How many pieces of string did Lin glue around her circle?

Snowman

Copy the snowman onto blank paper using a compass.

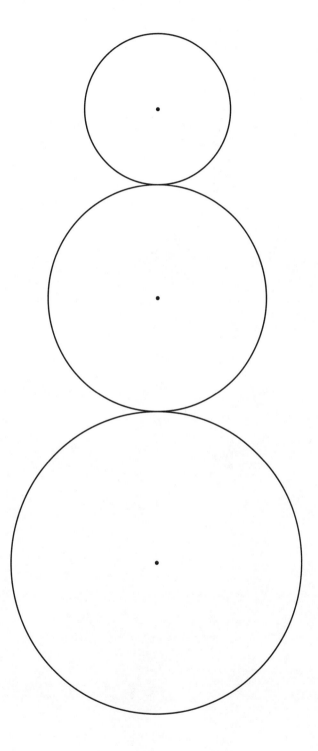

Make a Circle Graph

Nicholas and Edward surveyed students in the fifth grade to find out what type of pet they would prefer to have. They surveyed 78 students and organized their results in a table.

Type of Pet	Tally	Number of Students
dogs	ЖЖ ЖЖ ЖЖ ЖЖ ЖЖ II	27
cats	ЖЖ ЖЖ ЖЖ ЖЖ IIII	24
rodents (gerbil, guinea pig, hamster, mouse, etc.)	ЖЖ ЖЖ II	12
reptiles or amphibians	ЖЖ III	8
fish	III	3
birds	IIII	4

I. Nicholas and Edward want to make a circle graph to display their data. They need to express their data as percents. Complete the following chart. Use your calculator. Round each decimal to the nearest hundredth (0.01) before changing it to a percent.

Type of Pet	Number of Students	Fraction of Students	Decimal	Percent of Students
dogs	27	$\frac{27}{78}$	.3461538	35%
cats				
rodents				
reptiles or amphibians				
fish				
birds				

2. Cut out the small centiwheel at the bottom of the page. Use it to make a circle graph on the circle below using the data gathered by Nicholas and Edward. Make sure to add a title and labels to your graph.

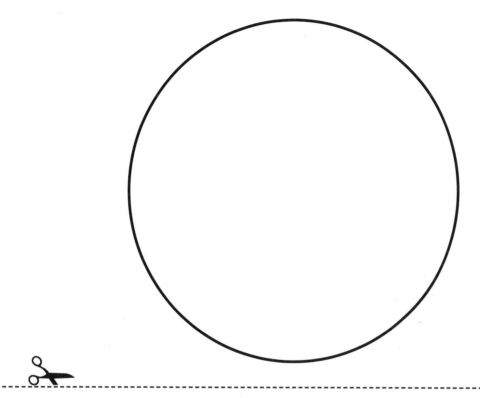

-- ✂ -

Small Centiwheel

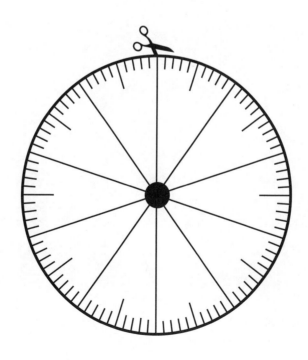

Unit 15

Developing Formulas with Geometry

	Student Guide	Discovery Assignment Book	Adventure Book	Unit Resource Guide*
Lesson 1				
Finding Area—Rectangles	●	●		
Lesson 2				
Rectangle Riddles	●			
Lesson 3				
Finding Area— Right Triangles	●			
Lesson 4				
More Triangles	●			
Lesson 5				
Perimeter	●			●
Lesson 6				
A Variety of Problems	●			

Unit Resource Guide pages are from the teacher materials.

⬤ Unit 15 ⬤ Home Practice

PART 1 Division Facts

Solve the following problems.

A. $480 \div 60 =$ **B.** $400 \div 20 =$

C. $800 \div 10 =$ **D.** $5600 \div 70 =$

E. $2800 \div 40 =$ **F.** $2400 \div 30 =$

G. $800 \div 40 =$ **H.** $900 \div 90 =$

I. $1200 \div 40 =$ **J.** $500 \div 10 =$

PART 2 Number Sense

Solve the following problems in your head.

1. Find the number N that makes each sentence true.

   A. $30 \div N = 6$ **B.** $N \div 6 = 7$ **C.** $24 \div 6 = N$ **D.** $36 \div N = 9$

   E. $N \div 8 = 8$ **F.** $16 \div N = 2$ **G.** $21 \div 3 = N$ **H.** $32 \div N = 8$

2. Solve.

   A. $40{,}000 \div 80 =$ **B.** $720 \div 90 =$ **C.** $3600 \div 6 =$ **D.** $270 \div 30 =$

   E. $48{,}000 \div 80 =$ **F.** $2000 \div 5 =$ **G.** $81{,}000 \div 90 =$ **H.** $3500 \div 70 =$

3. Follow the order of operations to solve each of the following.

   A. $5 \times 3 + 14 =$ **B.** $(33 + 7) \times 9 =$ **C.** $45 + 45 \div 9 =$ **D.** $7^2 + 8 \times 3 =$

PART 3 Fractions and Decimals

1. Write 3 decimals whose sum is 10 in two different ways.

2. Write two fractions whose product is $\frac{1}{4}$.

3. Solve the following using paper and pencil.

   A. $\frac{2}{5} - \frac{1}{4} =$ B. $6\frac{1}{4} + 2\frac{11}{12} =$ C. $0.34 \times 1.7 =$

PART 4 Area and Perimeter

You need two copies of *Centimeter Grid Paper* or *Centimeter Dot Paper* for this part.

1. Draw two different rectangles each with a perimeter of 20 cm. Find the area of each of your rectangles.

2. Draw a rectangle that has a width of 4 cm and a length that is twice the width. What is its area?

3. Draw a right triangle with a base of 6 cm and a height of 8 cm. What is its area?

4. Make a right triangle, an acute triangle, and an obtuse triangle with a base of 5 units and a height of 4 units. What is the area of all three triangles?

Name _____ Date _____

PART 5 Practicing the Operations

Solve the following problems using paper and pencil. Estimate to be sure your answers are reasonable. Write your answers to division problems as mixed numbers.

1. $26 \times 73 =$ 2. $3478 \div 7 =$ 3. $471 \times 60 =$

4. $1823 \div 21 =$ 5. $5077 \div 46 =$ 6. $67.2 \times 0.6 =$

Try to solve the following in your head without paper and pencil. Explain your strategies for Questions 7 and 9.

7. $14{,}034 + 160 =$ 8. $1270 + 330 =$ 9. $9099 - 100 =$

10. $0.5 \times 6400 =$ 11. $0.10 \times 150 =$ 12. $45 + 0.45 =$

13. $13 - 5.5 =$ 14. $23 \times 200 =$ 15. $1760 - 900 =$

PART 6 Building a Park

1. The city of Summerton is building a new park and playground. The location for the in-line skating and hockey rink must be paved with asphalt. The rectangular space for the rink has a length of 25 meters and a width of 15 meters. Each truck load of asphalt will cover exactly 100 square meters. A fence will be placed around the perimeter of the rink.

   A. What is the area of the rink?

   B. How many truck loads of asphalt will be needed to pave the rink?

   C. How many meters of fencing will be needed to enclose the rink?

2. 4900 square meters of the park will consist of a square, grassy field. Within this area team sports such as softball will be played. What will be the length of the side of the field?

3. The playground area will have swing sets and slides. It will be a rectangular area which measures 60 square feet. What could the length and width be if the sides have whole number lengths? List three possibilities.

4. There will be two triangular garden plots. One of the triangular areas has a base of 4 feet and a height of 3 feet. The other triangular area has a base of 3 feet and a height of 3 feet. What is the difference in the area of the two plots?

5. The park will have a snack shop. The counter in the snack shop is shaped like an L. Its measurements are shown in the picture. What is the area of the counter top? What is the perimeter?

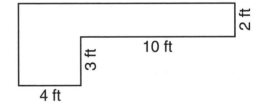

DEVELOPING FORMULAS WITH GEOMETRY

Finding Area: Review

Find the area of each of the shapes below.

Approximate the area of each shape below.

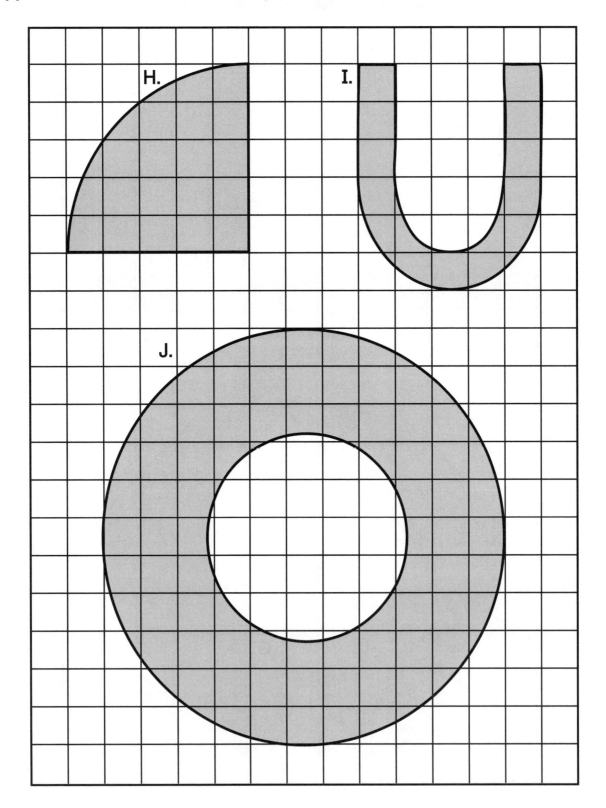

Finding Area–Rectangles

Unit 16

Bringing It All Together: An Assessment Unit

	Student Guide	Discovery Assignment Book	Adventure Book	Unit Resource Guide*
Lesson 1 Experiment Review	●	●		
Lesson 2 Bats!			●	
Lesson 3 More Bats!	●			
Lesson 4 How Many Bats in a Cave?	●			
Lesson 5 Pattern Block Candy				●
Lesson 6 End-of-Year Test				●
Lesson 7 Portfolio Review	●			

Unit Resource Guide pages are from the teacher materials.

Unit 16 Home Practice

PART 1 Division Practice

Use an appropriate strategy to find an exact answer for each of the following problems. You can choose between mental math, paper and pencil, and calculators. Mention which tool you used to solve each problem. Estimate to see if your answers are reasonable.

A. $8100 \div 90 =$

B. $18{,}000 \div 600 =$

C. $12{,}345 \div 5 =$

D. $40{,}824 \div 729 =$

E. $2509 \div 25 =$

F. $2410 \div 60 =$

PART 2 Fractions, Decimals, and Percents

1. A group of 18 students from Mr. Moreno's class went to a baseball game; $\frac{5}{6}$ of the students cheered for the home team. How many students cheered for the home team?

2. Blanca brought $15 to the game. She spent $7 on food. The rest of her money she spent on souvenirs.

   A. What fraction of her money did she spend on souvenirs?

   B. Write the fraction in Question 2A as a decimal. Round your answer to the nearest hundredth.

   C. Write the decimal in Question 2B as a percent.

3. The home team has won 24 out of their last 32 games.

   A. What fraction of the games have they won? Write this fraction in lowest terms.

   B. What percentage of their games have they won?

4. Out of the 18 students, 7 wore baseball caps to the game. Did more or less than 50% of the students wear a cap? What percentage of the students wore baseball caps? Give your answer to the nearest percent.

PART 3 Making Brownies

Below is a list of ingredients Manny uses to make one batch of walnut crunch brownies.

Walnut Crunch Brownies

4 squares chocolate

$\frac{3}{4}$ cup butter

$1\frac{1}{2}$ cups sugar

4 eggs

1 teaspoon vanilla

$\frac{2}{3}$ cup flour

$\frac{1}{4}$ cup walnuts

1. Manny only has 2 eggs at home. He plans to make half a recipe. List how much of each ingredient he needs.

2. Manny shares his original recipe with Felicia. She plans to double the recipe. How much of each ingredient will she need?

PART 4 Geometry

1. The circumference of a circle is 32 cm. What is the diameter of the circle? Give your answer to the nearest tenth of a centimeter. (Use the $\boxed{\pi}$ key on your calculator or use 3.14 for π.)

2. The radius of a circle is 4 cm. What is the circumference of the circle? Give your answer to the nearest tenth of a centimeter. (Use the $\boxed{\pi}$ key on your calculator or use 3.14 for π.)

3. The length of a rectangle is 6 cm. Its area is 54 sq cm. What is its perimeter?

4. The perimeter of a square is 24 cm. What is the area of the square?

PART 5 Practice

Solve the following problems using paper and pencil or mental math. Estimate to be sure your answers are reasonable. Give any remainders as whole numbers.

1. $63 \times 72 =$

2. $3089 \times 8 =$

3. $3090 \div 3 =$

4. $178.24 + 36.8 =$

5. $0.65 \times 46 =$

6. $17{,}346 \div 6 =$

7. $7\frac{7}{8} + 5\frac{2}{3} =$

8. $\frac{2}{3} - \frac{11}{18} =$

9. $\frac{4}{9} \times \frac{3}{4} =$

10. $\frac{3}{8} \times 80 =$

PART 6 The End of the School Year

Choose an appropriate method to solve each of the following problems. For some questions you may need to find an exact answer, while for others you may only need an estimate. For each question, you may choose to use paper and pencil, mental math, or a calculator. Use a separate sheet of paper to explain how you solved each problem.

1. On the last day of school Mr. Moreno collected his students' books. If each of his 22 students returns all of his or her books, Mr. Moreno should have 132 textbooks. How many textbooks did each student use during the year?

2. If a student loses a school library book, he or she must pay for the book. If the book is returned late, the student must pay a fine of 5¢ a school day for every school day it was late. Manny should have returned a book by March 25. It is June 2. If the book costs $3.95, is it cheaper for Manny to buy the book or return it and pay the overdue fine? Share your strategies.

3. Six students stayed after school to help Mr. Moreno pack up the classroom. He treated them to juice and popcorn. If Mr. Moreno bought 6 cans of juice from the machine in the teacher's lounge, it would have cost him 50¢ per can. Instead, on the way to school he bought six cans of juice for $2.69. How much did Mr. Moreno save per can?

4. On the way home, Blanca and Edward stopped at the park to play basketball. They both tried to shoot free throws. They both averaged 2 successful free throws out of 5 tries.

   A. If Blanca tried 20 times, how many free throws did she make?

   B. Edward made 12 free throws. How many times did he try?

5. Mr. Moreno decorated one bulletin board for next fall. Then he covered the board with butcher paper, so his decorations wouldn't fade. He has a bulletin board that is 2.4 meters long and 1.3 meters wide. What is the area of the bulletin board in square meters?

Experiment Review Chart

Experiment / Elements			
Main Variables			
Fixed Variables			
Variables Measured (units)			
Number of Trials			
Type of Graph			
Important Questions (Answers may vary.)			

Experiment Elements			
Main Variables			
Fixed Variables			
Variables Measured (units)			
Number of Trials			
Type of Graph			
Important Questions (Answers may vary.)			

Experiment Review

Name _____ Date _____

Experiment / Elements			
Main Variables			
Fixed Variables			
Variables Measured (units)			
Number of Trials			
Type of Graph			
Important Questions (Answers may vary.)			